WIRED FOR CONFLICT

WIRED FOR CONFLICT
THE ROLE OF PERSONALITY
IN RESOLVING DIFFERENCES

SONDRA S. VANSANT

Gainesville, Florida

Published by
Center for Applications of Psychological Type, Inc.
2815 NW 13th Street, Suite 401
Gainesville FL 32609
352.375.0160
www.capt.org

Myers-Briggs Type Indicator®, Myers-Briggs®, and MBTI® are trademarks or registered trademarks of the Myers-Briggs Type Indicator Trust in the United States and other countries.

CAPT, the CAPT logo, and Center for Applications of Psychological Type are trademarks of Center for Applications of Psychological Type, Inc., in the United States and other countries.

Printed in the United States of America.

Library of Congress Cataloging-in-Publications Data

VanSant, Sondra.
Wired for conflict: the role of personality in resolving differences /
Sondra S. VanSant.
    p. cm.
Includes bibliographical references.
ISBN 0-935652-68-X
1. Typology (Psychology). 2. Myers-Briggs Type Indicator. 3. Interpersonal conflict. 4. Conflict management. I. Title.

BF698.3V36 2003
155.2'64—dc21
203043971

Dedicated to Jerry, Laura, and Kevin,
my best coaches
on constructive use of differences
in conflict management

TABLE OF CONTENTS

ACKNOWLEDGEMENTS

ven a small volume requires a team to produce, and my heartfelt appreciation goes to the good folks at Center for Applications of Psychological Type (CAPT) for encouraging me to write this book and bringing it to reality. Jamie Johnson, research librarian, raised the issue with me for several years with reports of how frequently she received inquiries requesting such a volume and put in a good word about this to other staff. Editor Eleanor Sommer proved once again that two heads are better than one as she sharpened a phrase just the way I wished I'd stated it, often bringing needed clarity to concepts for readers new to the applications of personality type. Betsy Styron, CEO, was kind enough to read the manuscript and offer personal encouragement. Elayna Rexrode, project and production manager, coordinated it all into existence on a rushed timetable to be available for a scheduled workshop. I knew it was real when the excellent design work from John Amerson of Pro Ink appeared on my computer and even more imminent as David Forest, marketing director at CAPT, discussed his plans with me. What a joy to work with such a competent team.

Professional and personal friends gave generously of their limited time to read, edit, and talk ideas. Sandra Hirsh—friend, mentor, and role model—supported me past my hesitation at a critical time in the process, talking through options with the wisdom of experience. For reading drafts and offering perspective from their own types or endorsing the work, I am grateful to Terry Barnett, Vasudha Gupta, Frances Henderson, Jean McLendon, Steve Mullinix, Naomi Quenk, Charlene Scarborough, Dan Scarborough, Judy Schattner, Barbara Still, Paul

Tieger, Sharyn Warren, and David Williams. Diane Payne allowed me to use some of her fine perspective on type and conflict that she had written in our co-authored book *Psychological Type in Schools* as a part of chapter 3 of this book.

Closest to the work and to my writing efforts are those other VanSants who had direct input into the manuscript. Writing and mutual editing activities have become part of the multifaceted wiring of our forty-year marriage, and Jerry's ability to reduce complex ideas and verbiage to succinct yet interesting sentences remains for me an envied trait. His gift of a Sensing preference enhanced with excellent writing skills is second only to his support and patience through my writing efforts. Daughter Laura spent precious weekend time reading and making suggestions from the perspective of an exceptional journalist's ability to keep the reader engaged with few and well-chosen words.

Finally, I am extraordinarily grateful to those who joined me in workshops through the years and helped me to learn from their unique wiring how we need each other in this world because of our differences. I trust I have given accurate voice to their knowledge and experience.

Sondra VanSant
March, 2003

FOREWORD

s I sit here writing this foreword for Sondra VanSant's book, *Wired for Conflict: The Role of Personality in Resolving Differences*, I am aware of all the conflict brewing throughout the world at the moment of this writing. There is the current international conflict in the Middle East. There is conflict within our country as people try to make an *E Pluribus Unum* out of our different ethnicities, geographies, cultures, values, not to mention our differing politics and religion. In my work and personal life, I am often called in to help an employer-employee relationship, a team, or an organizational unit resolve conflict. Conflict, and the potential for it, is everywhere!

That is why Sondra VanSant's book is so important. Using her long and varied experience as an organizational consultant, a marriage and family counselor, a teacher/trainer, a psychologist, and a psychological type expert, Sondra gives us several fresh ways to look at conflict. She helps us to understand how we are *wired for conflict*. If we know that we are *wired* differently for conflict, we can use that knowledge to clarify and enhance our personal, interpersonal, and organizational relationships.

Adapting the theory of psychological types of Carl Jung, a Swiss medical doctor, Isabel Briggs Myers along with her mother, Katharine Cook Briggs, developed the Myers-Briggs Type Indicator® instrument (MBTI®). The MBTI types are Sondra's initial way to help us to see how we are each *wired for conflict* differently.

Myers used conflict as one of her motivating factors in the development of the Indicator. As an idealist with a practical bent, Myers thought that if we were to truly understand one another, we could choose to be amused by our different takes on life rather than be in conflict over them. She was right, we can.

Sondra VanSant shares Myers' intentions to use type knowledge to solve conflict. In personal correspondence, I asked Sondra what she hoped the benefit of this book would be for its readers. Sondra replied, "I want people to know that there is a 'personality type agenda' in dealing with conflict. People who know this can then validate their natural reactions to conflict rather than waste energy either being mystified by it or spending time defending it. When in conflict, they can redirect their energies more productively into understanding some of the others' natural type tendencies and move into an effective negotiation."

Beginning with the four psychological type dichotomies, Sondra gives examples of how each of the eight preference poles may approach a conflict. Those who prefer Extraversion may want to talk it out, while those who prefer Introversion may want to think it through. When conflict exists in giving and receiving appropriate work direction, those who prefer Sensing may want the specifics and details first, while those with a preference for Intuition may want to get the overall impression first. When there is a difference in how to give or receive feedback, Thinking types typically want to know what needs correction, while Feeling types may want to know what is going well first. And when conflict arises from different work styles, those with a preference for Judging may want a plan for a project, while those who prefer Perceiving may want the plan to emerge as the project goes along. Sondra offers vignettes to make the type differences clearer.

Additionally Sondra offers the reader "snapshot guides" (a decision-making model using Sensing, Intuition, Thinking, and Feeling) and illustrations of how a conflict might be played out. This review of the basics of psychological type gives the type expert, as well as the person new to type, a rationale to understand the different ways we are *wired for conflict*. Clearly knowing type provides a handy resource to better manage conflict!

Myers and Mary H. McCaulley, Ph.D., spoke to the importance of having good perception and good judgment when dealing with conflict. In the common vernacular this is fairly straightforward. One needs to gather adequate information and then organize that information according to appropriate decision factors. Sondra's distinctions are clear, concrete, and immediately usable. Readers will find *Wired for Conflict* to be a practical reference guide where they can learn how their specific function pairs may

☐ react to conflict,

☐ regard what is a satisfactory conflict resolution,

☐ approach a conflict where there are conflicting issues,

☐ want to communicate with and to each other while in conflict, and

☐ find themselves blindsided by conflict.

Unique to Sondra's book on conflict is information on type and body language. We all have experienced someone saying "I am not upset," while we may know that the opposite is true. Sondra uses the more easily observable combinations of Extraversion and Introversion combined with Judging and Perceiving to tell us how to read the body language while in conflict. She combines Extraversion and Judging, Extraversion and Perceiving, Introversion and Judging, and Introversion and Perceiving to give us some real-life clues.

Sondra is well versed in the literature of conflict and brings a new slant to the relationship of psychological types and the conflict management model developed by Kenneth Thomas and Ralph Kilmann, called the Thomas-Kilmann Conflict Mode Instrument (TKI). Understanding that *certain* types typically will have a *certain* TKI style can help both professionals and laypersons who know type and the Thomas-Kilmann model to anticipate how individuals will respond in a given conflict situation.

One of the best values of Sondra's book is her blend of type, conflict theory, and a seven-step model to effectively put this blend into practice. We learn how to use each preference dichotomy and function pair as we work through the seven-step model. Here is where the proverbial question, "Is this stuff really useful?" can be answered with an enthusiastic "Yes!" Sondra gives us seven solid steps, examples of wording, and specific type relevancies for each step.

Sondra's concern about the ethical use of type in dealing with conflict is most welcome and informative. Issues such as pigeonholing, intellectualizing, and using type knowledge exclusively to give oneself an unfair advantage in dealing with conflict are all cautioned against. Her choice of a Thomas Crum quotation from the book, *The Magic of Conflict*, underscores Sondra's values: "Resolving conflict is rarely about who is right. It is about acknowledgment and appreciation of differences."

Appendix B, "A Jungian Perspective on Response to the Stress Inherent in Conflict," is a positive tool both personally and professionally for learning about stressful possibilities inherent in all conflict. Knowing what kind of stress one might expect when in conflict and how one may respond "according to type" can be both comforting and supportive. It removes one's feeling of being alone with a jumble of emotions and restores a sense of perspective.

Sondra VanSant is a dear friend of many, a long-standing type expert, and a consummate professional. Her integrity, sense of humor, desire to help, and clear writing style make her words shine. Sondra's humor and warmth bring wisdom to this "touchy topic." *Wired for Conflict* will become one of those books that acquire the patina of use—tattered and earmarked. Thank you, Sondra, for giving us an insightful resource!

Sandra Krebs Hirsh
Minneapolis, MN
Author of
Work It Out:
Clues for Solving People Problems at Work

PREFACE

fight was the last thing my husband and I anticipated as we drove up the beautiful landscape to Haleakala's volcanic crater on the island of Maui. But before we'd gone little more than ten miles, we transformed what started as an adventurous drive into an exercise in frustrated fury. It began simply, as many conflicts do. On this, our first trip to the island paradise, we were soaking up as many of the sights and experiences as time and our energy would allow. We're hikers and had in hand a clever guidebook that not only listed the sites "not to be missed" but also gave helpful point-to-point mileage readings to locate precisely these and the various hiking trailheads. To make it work, you set your trip meter to zero and then monitor the distances as listed. Off we went leaving all self-awareness behind—my husband at the wheel and me poised to keep up with the numbers.

Quite easily I anticipated the first few stopovers so that we missed nothing. Then as the frequency of sites increased, I noticed I was feeling pretty edgy. Or maybe I noticed it when my husband remarked that he'd seen several signs for some sites I hadn't mentioned. Whatever. I think I suggested that we skip the book and enjoy the scenery, while he encouraged me to plug on with those decimal points. A half dozen or so switchbacks later not only did I realize I wasn't seeing much of anything because my head was buried in the book, but I had long since lost track of the numbers. And I was irrationally livid.

"But it is so simple," he said.

"Stop the car!" said I.

After a few minutes by the roadside gaining some equilibrium from silent sensual stimulation to eye and nose, we agreed, "We are having a type fight." We may have been slow on this one but once we tuned into the differences in our personality types, the solution was easy.

"I'll drive and you read the map."

Nothing else needed to be said. No blame. No need to feel totally incompetent. We both understood. Problem solved. Frustration gone.

Clearly, Carl Jung's model of psychological type (known as personality type by many) does not always produce such a simple solution. However, for my husband and me, understanding that our brains function differently, and therefore, the lenses through which we view the world can be quite opposite has turned many an argument into a collaborative process of creative problem solving. The transformation goes something like this:

□ *How could he/she even think that way!* to . . .

□ *Wait a minute—I think we're having a type fight* to . . .

□ *Of course, I can understand why I'm so frustrated and you seem so intransigent* to . . .

□ *How can we accommodate both our perspectives? And in our wisest moments* to . . .

□ *Here's an opportunity for my own development.*

This same thought progression occurs often in my work and other personal relationships—with much ongoing effort on my part. Being an Extraverted Feeling type, it's not surprising that I've sought opportunities to learn, work, and socialize interactively with others all my life. Of course, this frequent interaction has just increased my opportunities for conflict, and sometimes I think I have taken advantage of all of them!

Learning about psychological type more than twenty years ago was for me, like for so many others, a gift of life. Along the way, there have been people I consider wise teachers in my own understanding of using type in conflict situations for both creative resolution and for my own personal development. I was deeply moved many years ago when I heard Chandler Brown, founder and director at the time of Center Point, a Jungian organization and retreat center, talk about different types getting together in love relationships. She mentioned how couples enrich their relationships when they can say to each other something such as "Not only do you complement me, but you also model for me those aspects of myself I am in the process of developing. Because these aspects are less familiar to me, I will flounder with them over and over as I learn. I hope you can forgive me and allow me to keep learning."

Mary McCaulley, Ph.D., co-founder with Isabel Myers of the Center for Applications of Psychological Type, once reported to a group of which I was a part that Myers, author of the Myers-Briggs Type Indicator,® noted that we do not have to contrive laboratory experiments to develop and grow in our type. Life with all its normal activities is sufficient.

Diane Payne, my co-author of *Psychological Type in Schools* and principal of a high school with a strong peer mediation program, provoked deeper interest for me in how type has an impact on conflict. She suggested collecting data regarding conflict from different types that she then incorporated into our manual. Readers have found this material particularly helpful.

So with inspiration from people such as these, from my own counseling of work teams and couples and families in conflict, and through my own navigation of conflicts with others, I increasingly found applications for type. Consistently I saw positive results and continued to learn from people with types different from mine what helps and what hinders them in conflict situations. Gradually, this led to my conducting workshops on the use of type in conflict management and the opportunity to gather data in a more systematic way on how different types respond to conflict and effectively deal with it. This book draws on that experience and pulls together and applies information gained from the experts—people who know how individuals of their type communicate, learn, and negotiate most effectively.

The intent of the book is to offer this information in such a way that readers can learn more of what lies behind some of the seemingly enigmatic differences of human behavior, honor the strengths of their own natural response to conflict, discover fresh perspectives and strategies for negotiating disputes, and benefit from the personal development opportunity inherent in conflict.

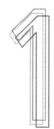

SECTION ONE

Winning and losing are goals for games, not for conflicts. Learning, growing, and cooperating are goals for resolving conflicts.

Thomas Crum
The Magic of Conflict

INTRODUCTION

All significant relationships reach a critical point when differences occur and we are faced with a choice. We can transform the conflict into creative resolution or we can choose to maintain the problem. We can work through the differences so that a mutual solution is found that enhances the issues we are trying to resolve, or we can succumb to a primitive fight/flight mechanism so that the conflict remains, intensifies, or is ignored. All too often we do the latter.

This book draws upon Carl Jung's principles of psychological type in an effort to increase the chances for a win/win resolution in conflict. (For purposes of this book, I will refer to *psychological type* as simply *type*.) A type-based approach actually uses differences to reach more creative solutions to confrontations in both personal and work relationships. The agreement reached can be more comprehensive, offer new perspective and vitality, and promote higher morale. (You, the reader, may be very familiar with type and its application to real life experience, or the ideas of type may be new to you. If this is your first encounter with type principles or you have limited knowledge, the first chapter will guide you through the basics in order to understand the application to conflict management and resolution in subsequent chapters.)

Conflict, of course, is inevitable for many reasons. Some conflicts are inevitable due to differences in family background, culture, experience, age, religion, roles performed, or gender. Other conflicts are inevitable because of the dissimilarity of personality types. Knowing the difference may determine whether the conflict reaches resolution or not. Unraveling and addressing the type issues in the conflict may solve the concerns. If the source of the conflict is other than type, understanding and honoring the type differences helps establish a productive dialogue by which other issues can be explored and possibly solved.

Innate Differences

Type is actually a brain model that, according to Jung, crosses gender and culture (Jung 1976). Some conflicts can even be anticipated due to differences in brain constitution. According to type concepts, our brains are hardwired for some conflicts to occur. Making constructive use of these innate differences in the way we use our mental processes allows us to take more conscious control of ourselves in conflict situations in order to work collaboratively rather than competitively with other people. Not only can the resolution process be made more efficient, but differences understood in the context of type become models for the expansion of mental functioning individually, as partners with others, and perhaps even culturally. We then gain more flexibility and wisdom for use with future decision making and conflicts.

What This Book Offers

This book will explain the tool of psychological type and provide applications for its use in dealing with conflict. The first five chapters provide information for understanding type and its impact on conflict situations. The remaining chapters apply this type knowledge to use in conflict management with a focus on creating win/win solutions.

☐ Chapter 1 provides an overview of the fundamental principles of type and explains differences in how we take in, process, and evaluate information.

☐ Chapter 2 applies this knowledge to conflict management using the fundamentals of type for basic understanding and application. A decision-making model for preventing conflict and "snapshot guides" to use when you are actually in a conflict situation are also included in this chapter.

☐ Chapter 3 expands this knowledge, explaining how interaction of the basic preferences occurs uniquely within each of the sixteen types.

□ Chapter 4 describes how type preferences typically affect the critical area of body language in communication and conflict management, making it easier to understand and behave in ways that increase opportunity for a positive outcome.

□ Chapter 5 describes a popular model for assessing and understanding different styles for handling conflict and how type tends to have an impact on which style is often selected when a conflict first sparks.

□ Chapter 6 combines all the type concepts and applications into a seven-step model for working collaboratively for a win/win solution that satisfies all parties. A process of collaboration has been shown again and again to produce the most creative and productive solution to most conflicts.

□ Chapter 7 suggests some situations in which type is appropriate to use. As useful as type can be in managing and resolving conflict, it may not be an appropriate tool for all situations. Included are some behavioral tips to observe for making this judgment.

□ The appendices provide more extensive information on two issues: a walk-through of the seven-step conflict resolution model between two parties in a business scenario; and a Jungian perspective on response to the stress inherent in conflict and how this may be manifested through the sixteen types when attempting to negotiate. Even though conflict is more stressful for some types than others, it is nonetheless stressful for all.

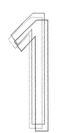

WHAT IS PSYCHOLOGICAL TYPE?

All too often, others with whom we come in contact do not reason as we reason, or do not value the things we value, or are not interested in what interests us.

Isabel Myers
Gifts Differing

any conflicts in which we find ourselves hit us out of the blue. We're surprised to wind up arguing, misunderstanding, or talking past each other when we and other generally reasonable people try to negotiate decisions, work for the same goals, or barter one thing for another. Little do we recognize that we literally may be on different wavelengths—brain waves that is.

Swiss psychologist Carl Jung concluded that at work in human minds are several pairs of opposite mental processes that we all use in situations requiring decision making. Furthermore, he determined that there are some fundamental differences in the way people prefer to use these opposites due to biological differences in the organization of our brains. He called these differences *psychological types* (Jung 1976).

The Myers-Briggs Type Indicator® Instrument

Jung's understanding of psychological type became more accessible when his German-language book on the subject was translated into English and was then discovered by an American woman, Katherine Briggs, who introduced her daughter, Isabel Myers, to Jung's concepts. Both women became lifelong students of Jung and his quest to understand human nature, and Myers worked for several decades researching and developing a means for understanding and applying his typology to individual and group differences. Her goal was an inventory to help people determine how their own personalities meshed with Jung's ideas of psychological type and how they might apply this knowledge to their daily lives. The result was the Myers-Briggs Type Indicator® (MBTI®) instrument now taken by more people around the world than any other psychological instrument of normal personality, with extensive research continuing across cultures around the globe.

Type, then, as put forward by Jung and Myers (Myers 1980), essentially involves four basic dichotomies (labeled *preferences* by Myers) working interactively in our minds.

Names of the Preferences

Extraversion–Introversion
Natural direction of our mental energy
(toward the outer or inner world)

Sensing–Intuition
Perceiving (what we pay attention to and
how we understand something)

Thinking–Feeling
Judging (how we make a decision about
our perception)

Judging–Perceiving
Which process we prefer to use when
dealing with our outer environment

While all of us use all of the preferences some of the time, each of us has an innate inclination for one of each pair. This preference is the one we rely on most often, are more comfortable with, and usually have developed the most skill using—much like being right- or left-handed.

Defining the Preferences

For those not familiar with the theory of psychological types, here are some brief definitions to help explain the concepts. Examples and more detailed explanations follow.

Extraversion–Introversion

First, Jung observed that people's minds are oriented toward and energized by two different environments. People with a preference for Extraversion are more oriented toward the outer environment and are energized when they connect actively with people, actions, and objects. Other people with a preference for Introversion are more oriented toward their inner environments and are energized through reflection on ideas and concepts.

Functioning well within either of these two environments requires that we balance a process of perception (coming to an awareness or perception of something) with a process of judgment (making a decision) about that perception.

Sensing–Intuition

The opposite mental functions for perceiving are called Sensing and Intuition and relate to what information is used to build a perception. The Sensing function focuses on specifics and realities about the present or past that can be verified, while the function of Intuition focuses on the big picture, hunches, and future possibilities.

Thinking–Feeling

The opposite functions for evaluating and making judgments are called Thinking and Feeling. The Thinking function evaluates with logic and analysis while the Feeling function evaluates with person-centered values such as fostering harmony and relationship.

Judging–Perception

The last pair was inferred from Jung's writings and added by Myers. It deals with which of the basic processes of Judging and Perceiving people prefer using when dealing with their outer environments. A person with a Judging preference wants things *decided* in the outer environment. A person with a preference for Judging tends to organize, plan, and schedule in order to bring about closure. A person with a preference for Perceiving wants to continue gathering information or develop options and tends to put off decision making until the last possible moment.

Understanding the Preferences

Understanding the richness of type requires understanding how all four of our preferences interact and how we make use of the less-preferred poles of each dichotomy. However, to grasp the basics of type, it is helpful first to understand each of the pairs and opposite preferences individually. Exploring these individual preferences is often the beginning of unraveling the type-influenced issues in a conflict situation.

Extraversion–Introversion
Orientation and source of mental energy

The direction of the energy of Extraversion is away from the person to the outer environment of other people, objects, and action. This engagement with the outer world replenishes mental energy for people who have a natural preference for this pole. It is known as an extraverted attitude, and Extraverts like to invest time and energy *interactively* working at solving problems.

The natural direction of energy for Introverts is toward the inner world involving reflection and internal mental processing. This active engagement with the inner world replenishes mental energy for people who have a natural preference for this pole. It is known as an introverted attitude, and Introverts like to invest time and energy *reflectively* working at solving problems.

> Mark, an Introvert who calls on clients much of his day, likes to recharge at the end of the day by briefly greeting his wife and then spending some time alone before preparing dinner with her. Betsy, on the other hand, is an Extravert who must introvert much of her day in her work as an attorney. She likes to recharge her energy by relaxing with a beverage and conversation with Mark before preparing dinner.

> Mark and Betsy engage in ongoing negotiation to prevent their differences from becoming a conflict of misunderstanding. As a compromise, sometimes they accommodate Mark's need and at other times Betsy's. Knowing that Betsy's desire for conversation with him is partially her way of recharging her energy helps him to postpone temporarily his own need for solitude. Understanding that Mark is not rejecting her company when he desires solitude makes it easier for her to postpone her own need for conversation until they begin

cooking dinner. On those evenings when he relaxes and talks with her before dinner preparation, she is then more understanding if he cooks more quietly or engages in less conversation during dinner.

Sensing–Intuition
Two ways of perceiving

Sensing is engaged by specific information that can be verified either by current experience through the senses or by knowledge learned in the past. It notices literal or tangible information. Sensing is engaged by what is real and has practical application, and it focuses on the present or past. It is concerned with the reality of "what is."

Intuition is engaged by global understandings—concepts, theories, symbols. It is more interested in the meaning of information than in the information itself. It likes to take seemingly unrelated things and connect them into themes or categories. Intuition is engaged by inspirations and insights that seem to come out of the unconscious, and it focuses on the present or future. It is concerned with the future possibilities of "what could be."

> Tina, who has a preference for Sensing, likes to give her staff specific instructions for tasks she wants accomplished, often with detailed steps for completing them. Some of her staff members find this quite helpful, but Maria, who has a preference for Intuition, finds it frustrating. She finds she has more interest in the task when she is given first an overall idea of what is to be accomplished and then is allowed to go about the task in her own way with no implication that she is to follow a set procedure for process or reporting.

> Once these natural differences were clarified and respected between Tina and Maria, Tina learned both to state the overall problem to be solved and some suggested steps for solving it, including the information she would like incorporated in the final reporting. Maria learned to include more information in her reporting in exchange for flexibility with her process. She understood that giving more procedural information was both natural for Tina and for some of her co-workers.

Both Sensing and Intuition can be experienced in an extraverted or introverted direction. Sensing in its introverted form gathers, orders, and files away internally information from what is already known and retrieves this data as needed for decision making. Sensing in its extraverted form gathers data from immediate experience with the outer environment as a basis for decision making affecting the present. Intuition in its introverted form is experienced as a hunch, insight, inspiration, or premonition—that sense of "I just know" without immediate awareness of how you know. Intuition in its extraverted form sees interesting possibilities in events and things in the outer world as it forms an overall impression of what could be.

Thinking–Feeling
Two ways of judging

Thinking involves rational evaluation based on logic and analysis. It focuses on objective data that can be examined for pros and cons and logical consequences. Thinking works for a conclusion that can be applied to specific situations or for a common principle that can be applied to any number of similar situations.

Feeling involves rational evaluation based on person-centered values. It focuses on personal values of harmony and relationship that examine the impact on people. Feeling works for conclusions that satisfy as many people as possible each time a decision needs to be made. People with a preference for Feeling often like consensus decision making.

> Roxanne, with a preference for Thinking, and Jacob, with a preference for Feeling, used to be at odds with each other at every meeting of the senior management team on which they served. Once a problem to be solved was raised, Roxanne and some other team members identified the objective facts of the situation and rather quickly reached a solution after analysis of the logical consequences of several options. Roxanne was visibly frustrated with Jacob's questions challenging what he considered to be their minimal attention given to all the stakeholders and their needs. To Roxanne the additional discussion was unnecessarily tedious and inefficient and thus costly to the organization. Jacob, in his frustration, began to lose morale and wondered if he wanted to continue working for a company that focused on the bottom line at the exclusion of human values.

A change came into their interactions when on several occasions they had to backtrack and revisit decisions. This was the result of unanticipated problems with both customer satisfaction and with employees who did not "buy in" to the decisions made by the managers. Jacob wisely engaged his Thinking function to do a cost comparison between the failed efforts requiring review and revision of their actions with the potential cost of investment in more extensive pre-decision investigation and discussion. Once Roxanne saw the logical reason for the investment of time and effort, she actively enlisted Jacob's views and opinion regarding the impact of the team's ideas on people. Each gained new respect for the other's different inclinations.

Both Thinking and Feeling can be experienced in an extraverted or introverted direction. Thinking in its introverted form evaluates and decides internally. People with a preference for this form of Thinking may not state aloud a decision already made. Sometimes they instead will ask questions of others to influence them to come to the conclusion they have already reached. Thinking in its extraverted form declares or applies a decision made to the outer environment, often without explaining how the decision was reached. Feeling in its introverted form evaluates on the basis of what creates and motivates inner harmony, even if the decision is in disagreement with the other's judgment. Feeling in its extraverted form seeks outer harmony so perseveres with decision making to foster total agreement between self and others.

Judging–Perceiving
Preferred process for dealing with the outer *environment*
Preference for a Judging process in the outer world means a preference for reaching decisions in matters that involve people, issues, and things around them. The Judging attitude focuses on bringing closure, and it strives for this using a judging function of Thinking, Feeling, or both. Persons who prefer this process in the outer world want matters decided and will organize, plan, and schedule in order to bring about closure.

Preference for using a Perceiving process in the outer world means a preference for keeping options open as long as possible in order to take in more information using Sensing, Intuition, or both. Perceiving likes to exploit each moment to the fullest before going forward into action.

It focuses on decision making only when the moment requires it, such as against a deadline. Persons who prefer this process in the outer world maintain flexibility and go with the flow of the moment until a decision has to be made.

> Seth was quite concerned when he heard that Larry was going to serve on a team charged with preparation for the re-accreditation of their human services agency. Seth had been appointed chair and had a preference for Judging. Larry, with a preference for Perceiving, had a reputation as an astute problem solver, whether it involved a matter concerning an individual client or the agency as a whole, pulling off at the last minute what had seemed impossible just days earlier. Seth respected Larry but saw him as a procrastinator. He also believed that the extensive written reports for which he was responsible and needed Larry's written input could not be accomplished at the last minute.
>
> A major conflict was avoided when Seth took the time to structure his own work on the project so that he knew at various points through the process what he wanted to have accomplished and what input from Larry was essential to get each phase completed. Larry agreed to meet these mini-deadlines in exchange for Seth's agreeing not to question him about how his work was progressing.

Developing Our Preferences

While we make decisions more effectively if we develop and use our natural preferences, we also make use of all of the opposites—just not at the same instant. In problem solving, if our mind is allowed to engage in its preferred mode, it is then easier to flex to bring in the opposite preference. But just as with right- or left-handedness, the environment in which we learn to use our preferences becomes important in their development. Ideally, the growing-up environment of family, school, and culture encourages the developing child to use his or her innate preferences so they become trusted and form the foundation for build-ing that child's unique mental strength and skills over the lifespan. Something of an internal disconnect can arise when a child is not supported in these natural inclinations.

Handedness again provides a good analogy. In the past naturally left-handed children were often discouraged from using their preferred hands for basic tasks such as writing and cutting paper. Pencils were taken from the left hand and placed in the right. There were no left-handed scissors or desks available. Talk to left-handed adults who had these experiences in their early schooling and you will usually hear that school was not a good place to be. Many people who could not easily adjust to using the nondominant hand report that they lost confidence in themselves because they assumed that teachers and school authorities must be correct. These people blamed themselves for the degree of difficulty in adapting. It came as great relief when somewhere along the line they learned that it was normal and okay to be left-handed!

Something similar happens when we first try to engage our minds with a *less-preferred* mental function or orientation of energy. We typically feel frustrated and inefficient and sometimes lose our sense of competence. Confidence and a sense of well-being come from both self-acceptance and from knowing we have done good work. The latter typically emerges from beginning a process with our natural preferences and *then* using those parts of our minds that require more intentional effort.

Summary of the Preferences

All of us use all of these sets of opposites; yet each person also has an innate preference or natural inclination to use one pole of each dichotomy over its opposite. These four preferences together form what we call our "type." To simplify things, Myers suggested the use of letters to represent the preferences.

E or I *(Extraversion or Introversion)*

S or N *(Sensing or Intuition)*

T or F *(Thinking or Feeling)*

J or P *(Judging or Perceiving)*

These preferences can be combined into sixteen combinations or four-letter types.

ISTJ	ISFJ	INFJ	INTJ
ISTP	ISFP	INFP	INTP
ESTP	ESFP	ENFP	ENTP
ESTJ	ESFJ	ENFJ	ENTJ

Interaction of the Preferences

Ideally, for problem solving to go smoothly and most effectively, our minds are best engaged first with the natural preferences and then stretched to include the opposites for a more complete perception and wiser judgment. Jung stressed that this separation and sequential use of all the functions is essential before integration (Jung 1976).

Type Development Over Time

In a perfect world, by the time we reach adulthood we will have had opportunities to develop skills with all the preferences and can appropriately select which preferences are best to use at any given time in any particular situations. Realistically, however, this does not happen. Developing all the functions toward the point of consistent effective use—especially when under stress—is a lifelong process known as type development. Because handling conflict well requires us to use all four functions, type development can be advanced by working through these disputes.

TYPE DIFFERENCES IN CONFLICT

Communication is the foundation on which all mutual problem solving rests. Differences between the types can be compared to language differences when trying to communicate—the more one learns to speak the other's language, the better the chance for understanding and problem solving. Using type when negotiating conflict assumes a person is willing to make similar adjustments to accommodate the other's preferences. The following pages are a kind of guidebook on the language of others.

Obviously, not all conflict is due to differences in type. However, extracting and sorting out type-based issues of the problem early in the disagreement is a productive way to begin managing the process for a win/win solution. The conflict may still exist but the acknowledgement and accommodation of needs arising from differences in type supports an environment for collaboration on the other issues inherent in the conflict. It helps to depersonalize the conflict. Even if one remains frustrated from type-influenced differences of needs, interests, and process, there is a sense of understanding and respect rather than an attitude of hostility.

Parts of this chapter are adapted from *Psychological Type in Schools* by Sondra VanSant and Diane Payne (1995 CAPT).

Extraversion–Introversion

Major Impact: *Differences in Pacing and Breadth of Focus*

Extraversion	Introversion
☐ *Likes a rapid pace*	☐ *Uses a quieter tone of voice*
☐ *Talks to facilitate thinking*	☐ *Often pauses to reflect*
☐ *May change direction when new information comes from the discussion*	☐ *Wants to focus*
☐ *May assume silence means agreement*	☐ *May use silence to indicate an unwillingness to disclose their thoughts and feelings*

Extraverts typically want to talk about a conflict right away whereas Introverts usually prefer to think about the conflict and take some time to consider the issues before discussing them. Because Extraverts are energized by engaging the outer world and enjoy the world of action and interaction, they often want to work out differences by talking about them. As they discuss the problem, they will formulate their ideas and beliefs about the situation. The first thoughts they voice are just that—their preliminary thoughts. *Inter*action takes them deeper into their thinking process, and if interaction does not occur, their thinking process may be curtailed. Further, Extraverts often do not end up where they began because new information and perspective gained through dialogue or experience is an important part of the process they use to arrive at their best opinions.

Introverts, on the other hand, are reflective and turn inward when faced with a conflict. They prefer to think about the situation in their inner worlds that provides them with energy before they share their concerns with others. Thus, others will be unaware of what they are thinking until they choose to share those thoughts. If this need for reflection is not accommodated, their thinking process is curtailed and their best thoughts related to the conflict will be lost to the process.

Since Extraverts want to settle their differences by talking about them, Introverts who may refuse to discuss the conflict or may stop talking before the conflict has been resolved often confound them. Extraverts frequently then assume silence means agreement or disengagement. For Introverts, silence may simply indicate they are not yet ready to reveal what they are thinking or feeling, particularly if they are not yet certain their perspectives will be treated with respect.

The fight/flight dynamic of our involuntary nervous system in the face of conflict elicits different natural responses from these preferences. Extraverts are inclined toward fight and Introverts toward flight, both behaviors that exacerbate the conflict, often producing a kind of two-step dance. One party will move in on the other who moves back, leading the first party to move in again and the other to move back, and so on.

Applying type intentionally can help resolve the impasse and engage the dancers in a flow of both dialogue and individual reflection. An Extravert can help an Introvert by acknowledging his or her need to reflect on the situation and by negotiating a period of time for this. An Introvert can help an Extravert by recognizing the Extravert's need to talk. When an Introvert does succeed in gaining a pause in the process to reflect, he or she should be willing to tell the Extravert when conversation can resume. Introverts also can become more willing to share their reflections.

Of course, no two people are exactly alike even if they share the same type. Asking what others need allows for these differences as well as shows respect for their uniqueness as an individual.

Clues to Possible Conflict

Some typical examples where conflict may be anticipated due to Extraversion–Introversion differences include the following:

Personal Life

Starting and ending the day. Extraverts will typically begin and end the day in conversation whereas Introverts prefer a more quiet time.

Dealing with shared decisions. Opinions firmly voiced by Extraverts do not necessarily reflect their final decisions. There is still room and probably desire for additional input. The challenge is for the Extravert to ask for it.

Interacting when an Extravert wants to engage and an Introvert needs time and space alone. The Extravert can respect the Introvert's response of "not now" and ask "If not now, when?" The Introvert can then negotiate another time and commit to being available.

Meaning of intimacy. Extraverts often believe intimacy involves time mainly spent interactively engaged. Introverts say that when quietly sharing individual activities side-by-side with someone you care about, a sense of intimacy is just as real.

Vacationing and leisure time. Differing needs for interaction as well as alone or quiet periods can be accommodated.

Allowing time for dialogue. Extraverts and Introverts require various amounts of "conversation." Develop the habit of "rounds" of discussion. Negotiate before beginning a talk how long that particular round will last and stick to it, agreeing on another time for the next round.

Organizations

Working environment. Introverts generally want quiet and minimal external activity to do their best work. Extraverts often need this environment as well when they need to concentrate. However, they also need frequent access to external activity in order to keep their energy and motivation high.

Meeting agendas. The use of, distribution of, and adherence to agendas varies with individuals and may depend on the purpose or importance of the meeting or process. Introverts often want more lead time than do Extraverts on discussion points or decisions to be made so they can reflect ahead of time. They also generally prefer minimal deviation from the agenda once the meeting is underway.

Meeting structure. Allow time both for discussion and reflection as new ideas or information emerge from discussion. Determine if a decision absolutely must be made immediately. It may be wise to postpone some decisions to allow further thought, particularly to invite the Introverts' best perspectives.

Learning

Introducing a lesson. Extraverts generally want minimal presentation of rationale or theory before trying something out. Introverts generally want a rationale or theory they can reflect on and understand before trying something out. Reaching a compromise on this one often helps. Provide some application with the introduction—such as some questions the learning will help answer or a "What's wrong with this picture?" story or incident.

Group or Individual. Schools often provide too little interactive time for Extraverts; organizational training programs often provide too little reflection time for Introverts. Effective learning models for all ages include a balance of both.

Domination of "air time." When ground rules for the learning environment are set, a discussion of how to assure that all types have equal opportunity to voice their questions and comments is important. Some groups supply sticky notes for placement on an "issues and questions" or "graffiti" board. Extraverts often like this arrangement so they can ask their questions or raise their points when they occur to them even if it is not aloud. Introverts often like this as an opportunity to ask a question or make their points more privately.

Sensing–Intuition

Major Impact: *Differences in Perspective*

Sensing

☐ *Addresses verifiable specifics*

☐ *Approaches a conflict as a discrete incident*

Sue was five days late with each of two reports last month.

Intuition

☐ *Addresses interpretation and meaning*

☐ *Seeks a theme by relating current conflict to other conflicts*

Sue is a chronic procrastinator.

The following activity accommodates Extraversion/Introversion differences in a two-party conflict. Each person takes turns wearing the "sender" and "receiver" hats.

Wearing the sender hat, a person (usually the one most concerned about the conflict) states his or her perspective, which should contain no more than two critical points. The receiver then paraphrases back to the sender what was heard, giving the sender the chance to clarify until he or she feels heard on those one or two points alone.

Roles are then reversed, and the new sender replies with no more than one or two critical points that are then paraphrased back by the new receiver until the sender feels heard.

Roles are then reversed again and the process continues with roles alternating as above until an understanding is reached.

Because Sensing and Intuition view different aspects of the same situation, conflict often results when people with opposite preferences seem to be talking past each other. Sensing and Intuition involve what people pay attention to and thus what keeps their interest.

Sensing focuses on the facts, details, and concrete aspects of the situation and trusts verified information. People with this preference tend to remember who said what, how long the discussion took, and the body language and facial expressions of the participants. They often remember specific data that support their perspectives on situations.

Intuition is much more interested in connections, relationships, and meaning and it trusts hunches and inspirations. Because people with a preference for Intuition focus on "the big picture," they may not notice the details or the specific order of events. Further, they process information differently from Sensing types. Rather than remember occurrences in a step-by-step manner, they respond to the totality of the event. Hence, Intuitive types may be unable to recall the specifics of what happened but are very clear about their overall impression of the event.

Playing off each other, Sensing types and Intuitive types can exacerbate the conflict as one uses a remarkable ability to recall detail and the specific order of events while the other focuses on the meaning of the events or uses an impression or a theory to support a point of view. One becomes frustrated with too much detail, the other with too much being read into the situation. As a result, they thus may define the problem to be solved quite differently. To listen to the interaction is much like listening to two people speaking two different languages and yet trying to engage in productive dialogue.

Clues to Possible Conflict

Some typical examples where potential conflict may be anticipated due to Sensing–Intuition differences include the following. In my observation, training and experience often alters whether any particular individual will respond initially from his or her Sensing or Intuitive process.

Eyewitness accident report. Sensing types offer detailed accounts stated sequentially whereas Intuitive types offer overall impressions with few specifics. If a response is given using the Intuition function, it is best to ask (without sounding irritated) for more details, if needed.

Instructions given and received. Sometimes offering two sets of instructions may be useful: one clearly laying out expectations in step-by-step form, the other giving the overall purpose and stating desired outcomes without instructions on process. This is particularly useful for young people or for others who do not yet know your style.

Directions given and received. Interestingly, people with either preference like a fair amount of detail if they must find an unfamiliar place and have limited time to do so. This is often forgotten by an Intuitive type for whom the place is known. At the same time, too many unnecessary details can frustrate both preferences—though for different reasons. Those who prefer Sensing want to read details carefully, assuming all might be relevant. Those who prefer Intuition become overwhelmed and frustrated with too much detail.

Performance reviews. The Sensing preference appreciates measurable specifics; a person with a preference for Intuition receives best an overall assessment first, and then finds evaluation of specifics helpful if changed behavior is desired.

Allocation of finances. Sensing types see money as a commodity to be spent prudently; Intuitive types view money as a resource and support for possibilities with less concern for prudence.

Who drives and who reads the map. The Sensing function focuses on as much information as possible that helps reach a destination most efficiently, often anticipating streets or landmarks as the route is followed. The Intuitive function often relies on a sense of direction or if using a map, looks for just essential data, sometimes losing concentration on the specifics.

Thinking–Feeling

Two aspects particularly affecting conflict

Since conflict often arises from differences in focus as Sensing and Intuitive types are beginning to describe their perceptions of a problem, steps can be taken early in the discussion to reduce this tension. This can be accomplished by asking what one's preference requires in order to understand the concerns more clearly.

For instance, the person with a preference for Sensing can say, "I hear you saying that there are unclear role definitions on the department's new project. It will help me understand your concern better if you can give me a specific example of where you've noticed this."

The person with a preference for Intuition can say, "I know the details you're giving me are important. I think I'll be able to follow them better if I can grasp the big picture first. Are you saying that . . . ?"

The Meaning of Fairness

Thinking

☐ *Seeks to find a solution or principle that can be applied to all equitably*

"Points will be subtracted from your day-late paper since that was the announced policy."

Feeling

☐ *Seeks to create a solution that takes individual circumstances into account*

"What happened that caused you to turn in your paper late?"

Thinking approaches issues from an objective point of view. People with a preference for Thinking will analyze situations, clarify the differences, and develop logically based strategies. They want to discuss the facts, not deal with the personalities involved. Clarifying differences and looking at things objectively are critical, as is keeping personal emotions out of the discussions. They search for the just and right thing to do, even if some people may be hurt in the process. Conflicts may arise more frequently over principles that are of more concern than how people feel. Fairness means applying the same principle equally to all involved.

In discussing a conflict with a Thinking type, one should pay attention to the choice of words used in discussing the conflict. For example, ask, "What do you *think* about the situation?" rather than "How do you *feel* about the situation?"

Feeling, on the other hand, is concerned with the personal factors that are creating conflict. People with this preference want everyone to get along, and they strive to create harmony, ideally preferring that decisions be made by consensus. They may blame themselves or others for conflicts and will sometimes sacrifice their own comfort and needs in order to see situations resolved. While they may feel resentment later, at the time of the conflict they often feel settling differences is most important. In some cases, if someone has treated them unfairly, they will tend to avoid confronting the person for fear it will create ill will. Disharmony is difficult.

In working to resolve a conflict with a Feeling type, a person should encourage the expression of values and feelings that are important in the situation. Ask questions such as, "What are you feeling right now?" or "What is of most concern to you about this?" Then begin the process of seeking solutions.

Acknowledging feelings first when discussing a conflict with Feeling types will allow for the validation of the values underlying the feelings and permit Feeling types to believe the other person understands something important to them. Allowing Thinking types to express what is on their minds first and to explain how they have analyzed the situation will result in Thinking types believing their ideas are valued.

Clues to Possible Conflicts

Some typical examples where potential conflict may be anticipated due to differences in Thinking and Feeling include the following.

Constructive criticism. Thinking types will often overtly critique with underlying appreciation unvoiced, whereas Feeling types will have difficulty hearing the critique unless appreciation is expressed first.

Joint purchases. Suitability based on objective criteria such as cost, use, reliability will be important to Thinking types. Suitability based on personal satisfaction or personal development will be most important to Feeling types.

Performance reviews. Thinking types want to know the bottom-line contributions, whereas Feeling types want bottom line combined with generous acknowledgement of personal effort and uniqueness.

Parenting. This is a tricky area where unconscious agenda can alter responses. However, Thinking types generally find it easier to apply limits firmly and equally to each child in the same situation. Feeling types are more likely to "bend the rules" depending on a child's particular situation.

Expressing intimacy. Thinking types often associate accomplishing helpful or needed tasks and being good providers as a way of demonstrating love. Feeling types may not connect these actions with love, preferring to give and receive personal words and gifts.

Listening to problems. Thinking types start solving the problem even as they listen. Feeling types listen first to connect with where the person is coming from.

A familiar conflict arises when people who have a Feeling preference have a problem and wants someone simply to listen. If they state this problem to a person with a Feeling preference they are likely to find someone listening to them with a view toward understanding how it is affecting the person with a problem—the natural response for the Feeling function. If they state this problem to a person with a Thinking preference they may find the listener starts helping them solve the problem right away—the natural response for the Thinking function. Frustration sets in for the Feeling type who feels perfectly capable of solving the problem and simply wants someone else to know what difficulty is being experienced. An unnecessary conflict is now underway, and the Thinking type may feel set-up. "You asked for my help and now you reject it."

Instead, Feeling types can let the other person know what their needs are. For instance, "I would like to tell you about a problem I'm having, and I just need you to listen." Or "I have a problem I'd like to ask your advice about." Even then it is helpful if the Thinking type will precede the advice with an understanding comment. "I'm sorry you're having to deal with this." Or "Yeah, that's tough."

It is important to point out that the Feeling function is not the same thing as having feelings. Emotions play a role in decision making for both Thinking and Feeling types—as a secondary response to an underlying way of making decisions. Thinking types feel frustrated when logical analysis is not being used in the process. Feeling types feel frustrated if the personal impact on people is not being given sufficient attention.

Feeling types, in particular, need to become comfortable asking for what they need. Both Thinking and Feeling types generally can accept that a particular solution is illogical. It is not always easy to understand why a particular solution does not feel right—i.e., what values are not being honored. This sense of discomfort often requires more time to determine what may have a negative impact on people or on one's sense of inner harmony. If Feeling types do not ask for this time, they may find it difficult to give the decision complete loyalty later.

Judging–Perceiving

> ### Major Impact: *Differences in Time and Focus*
>
> **Judging**
> - *Works for conclusion and wants to know when closure is to occur*
> - *Puts focus on organization and structure in order to accommodate closure*
>
> **Perceiving**
> - *Has an internal sense of timing which knows when the time is right for closure—timing which cannot always be anticipated*
> - *Focuses on process and making the most of each moment*

Judging types want judgments made in the outer environment and so are concerned with closure. They like to have situations planned, organized, and in control with a view toward bringing about closure. When confronted with a conflict, Judging types tend to assess the situation, choose a solution and implement it as quickly as possible. With this momentum toward closure, they may sometimes resist attempts at negotiation. Once a decision has been reached, they may be reluctant to re-open the discussion and consider alternative solutions.

Perceiving types value independence and flexibility and like to keep options open as long as possible in order to take in more information or consider more alternatives. Perceiving types tend to regard decisions as tentative and are likely to suggest changing the decision if a better alternative is proposed.

People with a preference for Judging may resist Perceiving types' needs to fully explore information about situations or possible alternatives before making decisions. Perceiving types with their valuing of process may appear to Judging types to be indecisive or less serious about resolving the conflicts.

To people with a preference for Perceiving, Judging types may appear to be overly aggressive and decisive because of their desires to complete undertakings and move forward to other tasks. They may assume Judging types want to exert control over people, tasks, and the environment. While this may, in fact, be true, Judging types also may be comfortable with someone else being in control as long as the situation seems structured to focus on closure.

Clues to Possible Conflict

Some examples of conflict situations that may be anticipated due to differences in preference for Judging and Perceiving include the following.

Organization of papers and materials. Judging types tend to use a system for organization others can often understand; Perceiving types tend to have random piles or collections and they individually know where something can be located.

Mutual work on a project. Judging types typically prefer to work with a clear structure for planning and implementation from the outset, whereas Perceiving types like to begin a project with less structure to see what emerges in the process.

Mutual goal setting. Goals developed by Judging types tend to be specific and firm. Perceiving types tend to prefer goals stated more generally and tentatively.

Co-Leadership. As leaders, Judging types tend to like to develop desired outcomes and then structure plans for their attainment. Perceiving types often prefer allowing outcomes to evolve from discussion and ongoing experience.

The rub comes when Judging and Perceiving types are working on the same project and the person with a preference for Judging cannot complete his or her responsibility without the work of the other.

What often results is that Judging types assume that all will approach the task as they themselves tend to do—with an organized approach from the beginning which focuses on the deadline. Perceiving types, however, are most energized to "deliver" at the last minute. So the Judging types get concerned that the Perceiving types will not finish their part on time or will be frustrated because the various steps into which they have organized their work cannot be completed without input from the Perceiving types. They then hassle the Perceiving types, which evokes irritation and resistance.

A helpful strategy is for Judging types to determine what specifically is needed from their colleagues in order to be able to complete each of their own steps. Then they can negotiate for some "mini-deadlines" along the way toward the final deadline, agreeing not to ask for input any sooner. The pay-off for Perceiving types for commitment to meeting these intermediate deadlines is more freedom to work in their own style.

Vacation arrangements. Judging types often can relax and enjoy themselves more when some plans are in place around which they allow for spontaneity. Perceiving types prefer making arrangements as opportunities present themselves, limiting upfront planning to essentials such as reduced-fare plane tickets.

Quick Reference Guide to Preferences and Conflict

Extraversion	Introversion
☐ Wants to turn outward and work out differences by talking about them right away or by taking immediate action ☐ May assume silence means agreement—or disagreement	☐ Wants to turn inward and reflect on differences before talking about them ☐ May use silence to indicate an unwillingness to disclose views at the moment
Sensing	**Intuition**
☐ Believes the facts and details of the situation are most important ☐ May frustrate others with memory for detail of who, what, when or body language and facial expressions	☐ Believes the meaning and the implications of the situation are most important ☐ May frustrate others by reading too much into a situation
Thinking	**Feeling**
☐ Likes to analyze the conflict from an objective point of view ☐ Likes to clarify issues and develop solutions ☐ Concerned with principles ☐ Focuses on solutions without placing blame	☐ Likes to analyze the conflict from a personal perspective ☐ Likes to consider peoples' feelings and produce harmony ☐ Concerned with person-centered values ☐ May blame self for the conflict
Judging	**Perceiving**
☐ Strives to settle the conflict as quickly as possible ☐ Might want to reach a resolution before all issues are addressed ☐ May be reluctant to consider alternative solutions after a decision has been made	☐ Suggests many solutions to the conflict ☐ Might want to keep options open for discussion longer than necessary ☐ May agree to a resolution but not stick to it if something that seems more expedient comes along

Adapted from *Psychological Type in Schools by* Sondra VanSant and Diane Payne (1995 CAPT).

Type Differences in Conflict

Quick Reference Guide for Problem Solving with Type

Extraversion

- Give time to discuss the problem.
- Since people with a preference for Extraversion like to solve problems by talking about them, the first solution presented may not be the final one.

Introversion

- Give time to think about the problem.
- Do not expect an answer immediately. They may prefer to put their thoughts and feelings in writing rather than talk about them.
- Encourage them to share their thoughts and ideas.

Sensing

- Focus on the specific facts and details of the problem.
- Be concrete, practical, and realistic in making suggestions for problem resolution.
- Present the problem clearly and concisely. Do not "beat around the bush"—come straight to the point.

Intuition

- Focus on the implications and meaning of the situation.
- Present solutions which are creative, innovative, future-oriented.
- Present the "big picture" when describing the problem. Do not get hung up on giving all the details.

Thinking

- Allow them to analyze the problem and present a logical perspective on the situation.
- Don't personalize the situation. Present the facts, be objective, discuss the issues and brainstorm possible solutions.
- Encourage them to express their views. Ask them, "What do you think about the situation?"

Feeling

- Ask how they are feeling about the situation or possible solutions.
- Allow them the opportunity to acknowledge their personal reaction to their perspective before asking them to move to logical analysis. Restate their position back so they feel "heard."
- Begin by talking about areas of agreement to establish harmony.

Judging

- Present the problem and suggested solutions in an organized manner.
- Recognize and acknowledge their need for closure.

Perceiving

- Recognize they like flexibility and a variety of options.
- Present several possible solutions to the problem and allow them to choose.

Adapted from *Psychological Type in Schools by* Sondra VanSant and Diane Payne (1995 CAPT).

Prevent Conflict by Problem Solving with Type

Many conflicts between different types can be averted if early in the problem-solving process intentional effort is made to incorporate a balance of all four mental processes.

Recommendations for effective decision making typically suggest that you should begin by stating the problem to be solved, collect as much information as you can, generate as many possible solutions as your imagination will allow, and once ideas begin to dry up, evaluate the alternatives for the best solution. Isabel Myers proposed that type fits very cohesively into this model. Gordon Lawrence, Ph.D., author, educator, and psychological type expert, has suggested that this process forms a progression of steps in a Z formation that I have elaborated on as follows (Lawrence 1993).

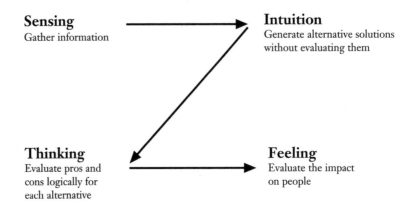

Sensing
Gather information

Intuition
Generate alternative solutions without evaluating them

Thinking
Evaluate pros and cons logically for each alternative

Feeling
Evaluate the impact on people

According to Jung and Myers, each of us has one step in the process that we find most interesting and that is where we choose to spend the most time and energy. A second step then attracts us and acts in tandem with the primary one. With these two steps, we tend to make decisions, generally giving little attention to the remaining two. Since the most effective decision generally involves conscientious use of *all four steps*, each type has two steps that represent potential blind spots in the process. These are the two mental functions that are less accessible to us consciously, suggesting that when making decisions we are wise to give extra attention to the intentional use of these functions and, if possible, collaborate with someone for whom these are their preferences.

It is not unusual for different types to be drawn into different aspects of the decision-making process and for this to be the source of much of the conflict. Fortunately, an understanding of both type and its use in decision making allows us to make constructive use of these differences by collaborating in order that all four steps are implemented adequately. This is known as making use of type in a dynamic rather than static way and is referred to as *type dynamics*.

The following table shows the order in which each type is most likely to use the four mental processes of Sensing, Intuition, Thinking, and Feeling. (The small letter indicates whether that function is more likely to be used in its extraverted or introverted form.)

A close look at the whole table shows that people with a preference

ISTJ	ISFJ	INFJ	INTJ
1) Sensing *(i)*	1) Sensing *(i)*	1) Intuition *(i)*	1) Intuition *(i)*
2) Thinking *(e)*	2) Feeling *(e)*	2) Feeling *(e)*	2) Thinking *(e)*
3) Feeling *(e)*	3) Thinking *(e)*	3) Thinking *(e)*	3) Feeling *(e)*
4) Intuition *(e)*	4) Intuition *(e)*	4) Sensing *(e)*	4) Sensing *(e)*

ISTP	ISFP	INFP	INTP
1) Thinking *(i)*	1) Feeling *(i)*	1) Feeling *(i)*	1) Thinking *(i)*
2) Sensing *(e)*	2) Sensing *(e)*	2) Intuition *(e)*	2) Intuition *(e)*
3) Intuition *(e)*	3) Intuition *(e)*	3) Sensing *(e)*	3) Sensing *(e)*
4) Feeling *(e)*	4) Thinking *(e)*	4) Thinking *(e)*	4) Feeling *(e)*

ESTP	ESFP	ENFP	ENTP
1) Sensing *(e)*	1) Sensing *(e)*	1) Intuition *(e)*	1) Intuition *(e)*
2) Thinking *(i)*	2) Feeling *(i)*	2) Feeling *(i)*	2) Thinking *(i)*
3) Feeling *(i)*	3) Thinking *(i)*	3) Thinking *(i)*	3) Feeling *(i)*
4) Intuition *(i)*	4) Intuition *(i)*	4) Sensing *(i)*	4) Sensing *(i)*

ESTJ	ESFJ	ENFJ	ENTJ
1) Thinking *(e)*	1) Feeling *(e)*	1) Feeling *(e)*	1) Thinking *(e)*
2) Sensing *(i)*	2) Sensing *(i)*	2) Intuition *(i)*	2) Intuition *(i)*
3) Intuition *(i)*	3) Intuition *(i)*	3) Sensing *(i)*	3) Sensing *(i)*
4) Feeling *(i)*	4) Thinking *(i)*	4) Thinking *(i)*	4) Feeling *(i)*

for Extraversion use their most dominant function most often in the outer world while those with a preference for Introversion use their most dominant most often in their inner world. (Check the table for your own type.)

Applying this information to the process of conflict resolution suggests that Introverts and Extraverts often may not be communicating with each other from their most preferred place. For example, an ISTJ team leader talking with an ENFP team member will most likely introvert his dominant function of Sensing and speak from his second function of extraverted Thinking while the ENFP will most likely speak from her dominant function of extraverted Intuition and introvert her second function of Feeling.

ISTJ   **ENFP**

In practical terms this means that the ISTJ will probably use his extraverted Thinking to make definitive statements about conclusions he has reached without indicating that using his introverted Sensing he has gathered and organized a good deal of information as a basis for making his decision. At the same time, the ENFP will probably give any number of ideas from her extraverted Intuition without indicating the deep core of values in her introverted Feeling that makes these ideas worthwhile to her. A conversation might go like this:

ISTJ: I've decided that we will spend the budget reserve on new software to upgrade our inventory system.

ENFP: I must admit I'm surprised. You asked us for our input on that decision and we all gave you at least six other department needs. I've come up with three or four others since then. *(To herself: He never pays any attention to what we say; I don't even know why he asks. We're a team in name only. I don't know why we even bother holding meetings.)*

ISTJ: It's already been submitted to the division head. *(To himself: I asked the group for input and then made a decision after analysis of the information they gave me. I'm unappreciated by the group, but at least we have an efficient, cost-effective department.)*

The problem of how to spend the budget reserve late in the fiscal year was viewed quite differently by these two types. The ISTJ was most interested in getting a logical decision made rather quickly that addressed the organizational needs of the department. His Sensing had been collecting and storing information in his mind on a regular basis for retrieval at the appropriate time to support his concern for greater departmental efficiency and increased production. When the deadline for use of the reserve was at hand, he has asked his team for additional information and assumed they had a similar full internal storage system that they shared completely with him when he asked for it at the meeting. The fundamental problem as he saw it was to take this information and make a decision.

The ENFP saw the reserve as an opportunity for new ideas that would benefit the department and its mission beyond those planned for when the budget was devised. Her extraverted Intuition was interested in generating as many ideas as possible, particularly those which supported increased creativity on the part of team members and which her introverted Feeling believed would address the much-needed boost to morale. To her, there had hardly been enough time allowed in the one meeting to generate sufficient ideas. The fundamental problem as she saw it was one of low morale and the need for exploration of possibilities for solving this.

The following table indicates the natural priority given to the decision-making steps by each of the types. (Again, check your own type.)

Relative Emphasis of Functions in Problem Solving

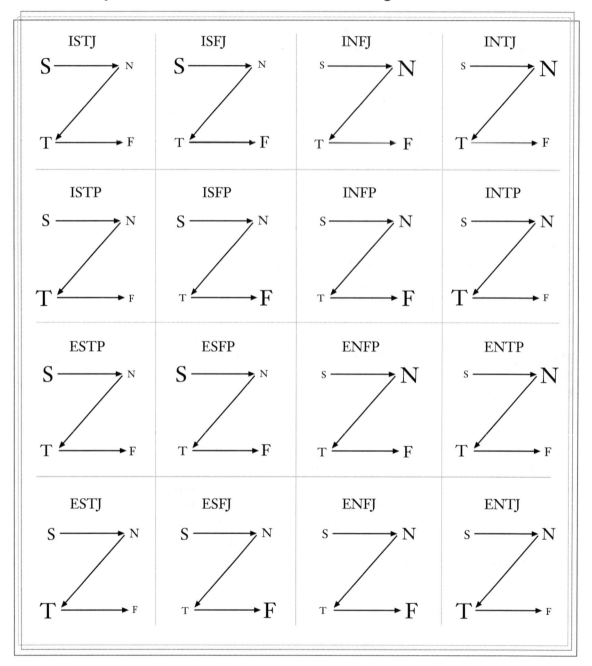

Had the ISTJ and ENFP in our example understood type and type dynamics, they would have recognized how they were missing the significant point that they actually shared a common purpose. Both wanted to increase the productivity of the department, but they focused on different aspects of the issue. In a meeting together, they and other team members could have both discussed and reflected on the processes of Sensing, Intuition, Thinking, and Feeling and collaborated to find a solution that addressed both increased organizational efficiency and higher morale.

Because at some level, the mind acknowledges the importance of all four processes, putting trust and confidence in natural preferences makes it easier to pay more attention to the areas in danger of being shortchanged. That is how the "opposites" are developed over time and satisfy the natural desire of the psyche for wholeness.

Together, perception and
judgment, which make up
a large portion of people's
total mental activity, govern
much of their outer
behavior.

Isabel Myers
Gifts Differing

TYPE GROUPS AND CONFLICT

Working with only the four basic dichotomies as separate dimensions is useful in resolving conflict but misses the full interplay of the preferences. An ESFJ type is more than the sum of Extraversion plus Sensing plus Feeling plus Judging. Putting all the preferences together into a dynamic whole type is a kind of code as to how a person is most likely to function in totality.

Realistically, effective problem solving becomes possible when we have and use both one well-developed Perceiving function (Sensing or Intuition) and one well-developed Judging function (Thinking or Feeling) and use the opposite preferences in a supportive role. Yet it may not be practical to learn how sixteen different types tend to operate in conflict. So to obtain a workable compromise without sacrificing all of the richness of a whole type, it is possible to reduce the sixteen combinations to four: ST, SF, NT, NF—known as "function pairs."

What follows is information collected from people representing all sixteen types and then clustered by function pairs. I consider these people experts in their own types in a way I, with a different type, can never be. Presented in categories by commonly shared preferences for perceiving and judging, these sections give quick and practical references for both self-understanding and better understanding of others when facing conflict if their types are known. If you do not know their types but have developed a "working hypothesis" of their types from their verbal cues, you will find some suggestions for communicating more effectively with types other than your own.

Each section highlights a basic first reaction when faced with conflict, what criteria define a satisfactory resolution, how conflict is approached naturally, what is needed from others for most effective communication, potential blind spots the type may have in conflict situations, and tips for people with those preferences who want to increase their effectiveness in conflict management and resolution. There is also a brief section on some variation among the four types belonging to each function pair.

SENSING THINKING TYPES (ST)

Combines the specificity, ordering, realism, and practicality of Sensing with the logical and analytical evaluation of Thinking.

Reactions to Conflict

- ☐ See conflict as a normal part of life to be dealt with realistically and practically
- ☐ Confront it
- ☐ Respond directly and objectively
- ☐ Work out the problem in the most logical and efficient way possible
- ☐ Solve the conflict as soon as possible

Characteristics of Satisfactory Resolutions

- ☐ Logical
- ☐ Practical
- ☐ Realistic
- ☐ Workable
- ☐ Reasonable
- ☐ Efficient
- ☐ Results oriented
- ☐ History of effectiveness

Approaches to Solving Conflict

- ☐ Respond directly and objectively
- ☐ Logically try to work out the problem
- ☐ Quickly make a judgment, involving others if necessary
- ☐ Take action on the judgment quickly

Communication Needs

- ☐ Direct approach from the other party related to issues and relevant information
- ☐ Succinct verbal discussion focused on the issues
- ☐ Practical, realistic data
- ☐ Options for solutions which can be accomplished quickly
- ☐ Discussion in a calm manner
- ☐ Opportunity to make comments and give reactions following presentation of facts by the other party

**Tips for Sensing
Thinking Types to
Resolve Conflict
Effectively**

Make it your task to
approach each conflict as
an opportunity to learn
something.

Note physical tension in the
body and relax it.

Ask other stakeholders how
the situation affects them.

Express some
understanding of
their answers.

Suspend making a decision
until as many options as
possible have been put
forward for discussion.

Resist acting unilaterally.

Potential Blind Spots

☐ Awareness and affirmation of own and others' emotions in the
conflict

☐ Might tell or act more than listen

☐ Might not consider or discuss all the possible alternatives

☐ Might decide on a solution too quickly, possibly missing
opportunity for a more creative solution that would satisfy all
stakeholders

☐ Might decide on a solution too independently and lose support
from other stakeholders

☐ Might not express appreciation before offering critique

☐ Might create conflict by offering suggestions for problem solving
when the other party simply wants a listening ear

Variations Among Sensing Thinking Types

	ESTJ	ESTP
Particular contribution to the conflict-resolution process	☐ Momentum for making tough-minded decisions ☐ A plan of implementation	☐ Resourcefulness and ability to quickly determine reality ☐ Momentum toward action
What someone is likely to hear or see	☐ A logical judgment succinctly stated and firmly adhered to ☐ Calculated risk-taking	☐ Some trial and error approaches to solving the problem ☐ Uninhibited risk-taking
What someone might not hear	☐ The analysis of current data combined with data from past experience that is the basis for the decision	☐ The internal process of structuring and analyzing data to produce a solution
	ISTJ	**ISTP**
Particular contribution to the conflict-resolution process	☐ Momentum to collect and analyze data thoroughly before deciding ☐ A plan of implementation geared toward sustainability	☐ Focus on reality which is distilled to simplest terms ☐ Momentum for a solution which produces tangible results.
What someone is likely to hear or see	☐ Concentrated action toward solving the problem	☐ Attention or action toward a hands-on solution
What someone might not hear	☐ The analysis of current data combined with data from past experience which is the basis for their action	☐ The logical process by which they determined their solution

SENSING FEELING TYPES (SF)

Combines the specificity, realism, ordering, and practicality of Sensing with the person-centered evaluation process of Feeling.

Reactions to Conflict

- Discomfort
- See the negative impact on others
- Want to work out the problem so that everyone involved in the process is comfortable with the solution

Characteristics of Satisfactory Resolutions

- Beneficial to people
- Equitable
- Practical and concrete
- Reached by consensus
- Produce win/win solutions

Approaches to Solving Conflict

- Consider people's feelings and needs
- Narrow options by mutual consent
- Treat people kindly
- Show respect
- Avoid criticizing
- Focus on what each person wants to happen
- Look for solutions that seem practical and expedient
- Brainstorm solutions together and choose a solution that satisfies all parties

Communication Needs

- Consideration of feelings
- Sense of being respected and treated kindly
- Open, honest approach without blame or criticism
- Discussion of the conflict with indication of a willingness to work it out
- Time allowed for individual processing and reflection
- Focus on the concrete and practical rather than hypotheses
- Minimal brainstorming
- Processing for consensus
- Opportunity to give information on how people might be affected

Possible Blind Spots

☐ May take the issues personally
☐ May accommodate others' needs too quickly for the sake of harmony
☐ May later resent accommodation made too quickly
☐ May ignore own feelings as clues to the nature of the problem
☐ May ask questions that are actually meant as statements
☐ May not see the big picture
☐ May exaggerate the effect of hurt feelings
☐ May appear manipulative to others due to indirectness

Tips for Sensing Feeling Types to Resolve Conflict Effectively

Practice handling conflict directly rather than indirectly.

Clarify your understanding of the big picture once you have gathered information.

Develop objectivity and see conflict as a problem to be solved rather than as personal criticism.

Receive and review information before accepting or rejecting it.

Suspend making a decision until as many questions as possible have been put forward for discussion, even if some of the options seem impractical.

Variations Among Sensing Feeling Types

	ESFJ	**ESFP**
Particular contribution to the conflict-resolution process	☐ Perseverance to find a solution all are comfortable with ☐ Strong commitment to goals agreed upon	☐ Momentum to move to practical action as soon as possible ☐ Resourcefulness and adaptability
What someone is likely to hear or see	☐ Intensity of voice	☐ A casual approach to the process
What someone might not hear	☐ Their keen awareness of the impact of conflict on the lives of those involved and their passionate concern for bringing harmony to the situation	☐ The depth of desire to create harmony for themselves and others
	ISFJ	**ISFP**
Particular contribution to the conflict-resolution process	☐ Perseverance on actions they believe will help change the situation causing conflict ☐ Memory for information helpful to the process	☐ Quiet, keen observation of the impact of the process on people, including non-verbal clues ☐ Sense of humor at unexpected moments
What someone is likely to hear or see	☐ Individual action with little verbal expression	☐ Action undertaken as an adventure
What someone might not hear	☐ Their deep desire to make life harmonious for the others involved in the conflict	☐ Their deep commitment to protecting their own and others' freedom and comfort

INTUITIVE FEELING TYPES (NF)

Combines the global, future-possibility perspective of Intuition with the person-centered evaluation process of Feeling.

Reactions to Conflict

□ May feel misunderstood or surprised that there is a conflict

□ May initially feel hurt and get into a depressed mood

□ Immediate response is to regard holding onto a personal value or maintaining the relationship as more important than the conflict issue

□ Prefer to ignore or avoid the conflict unless there is a collision of values

□ Accommodate the other if it doesn't conflict with personal values

□ See it as an opportunity for growth and development both intrapersonally and interpersonally

□ Believe reaching a mutual resolution will help the corporate body or relationship to grow and develop and function more effectively

Characteristics of Satisfactory Resolutions

□ Harmonious

□ Focused on people

□ Insightful

□ Developed by consensus

□ Win/win solution or at least a compromise

Approaches to Solving Conflict

□ Focus on person-centered values of relationship and harmony

□ Find points of agreement and work toward consensus

□ Seek creative solutions

□ Allow for personal growth and insight

□ Encourage input from others

□ Cooperate, communicate, compromise

Communication Needs

□ Evidence of concern for the relationship

□ Sense of warmth and support

□ Respectful listening with paraphrasing of what was heard

Handle conflict directly with the person involved rather than indirectly.

Initially take information at face value rather than attach meaning to it.

Pay attention to specific data as well as the big picture.

Temporarily suspend making judgment about information or others' opinions while exploring workable options.

Step into an observer role when personalizing the situation gets in the way of dialogue.

Trust your insights and explore them even if others do not agree with them.

Practice conciseness and clarity of speech.

Ask for time to reflect to gather and clarify your thoughts, perhaps writing them down.

☐ Opportunity to clarify meaning and intent until he or she feels understood
☐ Acknowledgment of values important to the person
☐ Affirmation of strengths before critical concerns are raised
☐ Calm, positive interaction

Potential Blind Spots

☐ May initially only talk around the edges of the conflict
☐ May ask questions actually intended as statements, confusing or frustrating the other party
☐ May talk to others about the problem rather than directly to the person involved
☐ May not be aware that indirectness can appear as manipulation to others
☐ May not seek or hear all the relevant facts
☐ May decide too quickly on an insight as the right solution
☐ May take personally comments meant impersonally
☐ May exaggerate the effect of hurt feelings
☐ May resent later an accommodation made too quickly
☐ May not state thoughts succinctly and therefore be difficult for others to track

Variations Among Intuitive Feeling Types

	ENFJ	**ENFP**
Particular contribution to the conflict-resolution process	☐ Strive to have all stakeholders talk out the conflict to reach a decision ☐ Keen awareness of how alternative solutions are likely to affect people individually	☐ Strive to have as many options as possible put on the table before a decision is made ☐ Push to consider the unproven
What someone is likely to hear or see	☐ Quick solutions that sound more focused on empathy or sociability than objective problem solving	☐ A possibility in every idea put on the table
What someone might not hear	☐ Their developing private insights on how the conflict can be resolved	☐ The decisions they are making regarding which solution they will ultimately commit to
	INFJ	**INFP**
Particular contribution to the conflict-resolution process	☐ Keen awareness of insights from the unconscious ☐ Perseverance to make their creative vision a reality	☐ Firmness of focus on person-centered values ☐ Quiet observation and summarizing of issues
What someone is likely to hear or see	☐ Intensity and impetus to have a decision made based on people's needs	☐ Nonjudgmental attention to the other person's concerns
What someone might not hear	☐ The observation of people issues in the current situation and how they relate to the larger human condition	☐ Evaluation of others' concerns against the criteria of their personal values

INTUITIVE THINKING TYPES (NT)

Combines the global, future possibility perspective of Intuition with the logical, analytical evaluation of Thinking

Reactions to Conflict

☐ See conflict as a challenge and an opportunity for innovation and change
☐ Believe conflict is a problem to be solved that leads ultimately to progress
☐ Prefer independent problem solving, involving others only as necessary

Characteristics of Satisfactory Resolutions

☐ Fair and just
☐ Logical
☐ Creative
☐ Innovative

Approaches to Solving Conflict

☐ Objectively analyze the situation, avoiding personalizing of the concerns
☐ Clarify the issues and principles at stake
☐ Determine all sides of an issue
☐ Consider pros and cons of the situation
☐ Use reasoning and logic in a problem-solving approach
☐ Determine a solution that can be applied equitably to any number of situations

Communication Needs

☐ Focus on the big picture of principles initially
☐ Willingness to strategize and consider multiple alternatives
☐ Willingness to try something new and different
☐ Direct and calm discussion
☐ Reasons explained with underlying principles
☐ Confrontation in private rather than in public

Potential Blind Spots

- ☐ May minimize the significance of personal feelings of self and others to the conflict
- ☐ May not understand how communication intensity might be intimidating to others
- ☐ May see argument as objective debate while others may take it as personal criticism
- ☐ May discount too quickly solutions that seem more people-focused than issue-focused
- ☐ May put the need to be right over the need for common understanding
- ☐ May have a tendency to control the process rather than collaborate
- ☐ May decide too quickly
- ☐ May create conflict by offering suggestions for problem solving when the other party just wants a listening ear

Tips for Intuitive Thinking Types to Resolve Conflict Effectively

Develop awareness of emotions of self and others in conflict.

Become aware of bodily sensations such as muscle tension as a clue to own emotions.

Ask others what they are feeling and affirm their answers.

Pay attention to specific information after discerning the global issues.

Avoid discounting, without consideration, solutions that have worked in the past.

Take advantage of the opportunity for empathic listening and collaboration.

Variations Among Intuitive Thinking Types

	ENTJ	**ENTP**
Particular contribution to the conflict-resolution process	☐ Drive for a decision in order to structure the attainment of broad goals ☐ Momentum to move forward once a solution is reached	☐ A wealth of creative ideas ☐ Energy to make what seems impossible as potentially doable with a little adaptation
What someone is likely to hear or see	☐ A firm decision not easily re-opened for discussion once made	☐ A momentum for change "for the sake of change"
What someone might not hear	☐ The numerous ideas they have explored internally for fairness and justice	☐ The internal categorizing and analysis of ideas presented even as new ideas are introduced

	INTJ	**INTP**
Particular contribution to the conflict-resolution process	☐ Ability to see a vision of the future ☐ Drive to realize their vision in the real world	☐ Interest in exploring complex ideas from every angle ☐ Tendency to ask tough questions to challenge the status quo
What someone is likely to hear or see	☐ Articulation of a complex systemic solution to a problem	☐ Critique of every solution introduced
What someone might not hear	☐ The vision of the ideal believed possible	☐ The internal principle at stake in the discussion

You never get a second
chance to make a first
impression

Popular Poster Quote
(Source Unknown)

IMPACT OF TYPE ON BODY LANGUAGE

very thought we have produces a physical and emotional response, and our bodies communicate a message even before we begin to speak. The visual image displayed by people engaged in conflict is first to convey to the other how the discussion is likely to proceed. Inconsistency between non-verbal expression and the words spoken is a sure way to lose credibility and create distrust or skepticism in a conflict-resolution process.

Experience makes it clear, however, that different types prefer different body language when negotiating conflict. Becoming aware of these possible differences enables us to take more conscious control of our own behavior to increase the likelihood of a positive outcome.

The Pairs of E–I and J–P

All of the preferences have an impact on body language. However, in my experience, the Extraversion–Introversion and Judging–Perceiving dichotomies particularly influence how people use their bodies and the physical space around them in working through conflict with others. Since Extraversion and Introversion pertain to direction of mental energy, it follows that people with preferences for Extraversion are more likely to want to handle conflict interactively and directly, using a wider span of physical space. Those with a preference for Introversion are more likely to want to reflect on the situation and perhaps attempt indirectly or more individually to resolve the issues, using a more focused use of space.

Since the attitudes of Judging and Perceiving have different purposes for the use of time spent in the outer environment, nonverbal expression typically reflects these differences. Judging structures time with a focus on bringing about closure. Perception wants to make the most of each moment, living each to its fullest. Combined in pairs, these preferences influence nonverbal tendencies in the following ways. (Keep in mind that, as with all type descriptions, these are not absolutes for any individual since these tendencies are affected by a person's own experiences and influences.)

Extraversion and Judging (EJ)
☐ Sit or stand in close proximity
☐ Face the other directly
☐ Maintain direct eye contact
☐ Punctuated hand movement for emphasis
☐ Body position leaning forward

Extraversion and Perceiving (EP)
☐ Much room to use large motions
☐ Freedom to stand, sit, or move around while talking
☐ Some eye contact but freedom to break it in order to move around
☐ Expansive hand motions for emphasis

Introversion and Judging (IJ)
☐ Enough distance to avoid physical touching
☐ May like a physical barrier between participants
☐ Much breaking of eye contact or a "glazing" over of the eyes when reflecting
☐ Understated hand movement

Introversion and Perceiving (IP)
- ☐ Informal stance
- ☐ Eye contact less important; may often look away except when making a point
- ☐ Little movement of hands and body
- ☐ No touching unless the relationship is very personal

Additional Points

Effect of Minor Adjustments

Type knowledge as a language is useful when we learn to understand and accept behavior of someone with preferences different from our own. This knowledge becomes particularly powerful when we learn to adapt our own behavior to speak to some degree the language of the other, recognizing that the expectation is not that we will be as fluent as the other. Making a few adjustments in our own natural styles, similar to learning a few phrases in another's language, goes a long way toward facilitating mutual understanding and cooperation.

Use of Touch

Comfort levels with touching are different even within each type. It is a good idea to check out the other person's comfort with touch before including this behavior in conflict resolution discussion. If you have a close personal relationship with the other person you can ask. Otherwise, stay on the side of caution unless the other person uses touch first.

Impact of Culture

Cultural influences have great impact on how one behaves in interpersonal situations. These may include different expectations depending on one's family, social, or power position with another or with someone of a different gender or age. In some cultures, for instance, direct eye contact is considered impolite and intrusive, as is direct verbalizing of differences or certain body postures that may convey inappropriate meaning during a conversation. When a person is in this situation, he or she typically adapts both verbal and nonverbal language (and the expression of type) to conform to these expectations. From my own experiences of living in other cultures, I recommend accommodation to known cultural norms first, and then gradually observing individual body and language cues that suggest ways an individual may uniquely express himself or herself within the culture.

Knowledge of and acceptance of one's own natural preferences can make it less difficult to adapt either to another culture or to another's preference different from one's own. Honoring and adapting to another's preference fosters the process of conflict resolution and has the added benefit of providing practice and development of one's own less-preferred mental functions.

Conflict is simply the
condition in which people's
concerns—the things they
care about—appear to be
incompatible.

Kenneth Thomas
Introduction to Conflict
Management

TYPE AND CONFLICT
MANAGEMENT STYLES

enneth Thomas and Ralph Kilmann developed one approach to understanding conflict-handling styles that has been used to research the style most used by each of the types. Using a model developed earlier by Robert Blake and Jane Mouton (1964) for categorizing management styles, Thomas and Kilmann (Thomas 2002) identified two dimensions of behavior involved in managing conflict with another party: concern for one's own interests and concern for the other person's interests. They labeled these Assertiveness and Cooperativeness, respectively. Depending on the degree to which a person proportions his or her energy into each of these dimensions, one of the styles will be engaged (see figure 5.1, page 54).

According to this model none of the styles are inherently good or bad. Each is appropriate for some situations and each is also inappropriate or less effective for other situations.

Competing. Behavior is based on a high attempt to satisfy one's own interests and a low attempt to satisfy the other party's interests. A person chooses to use power to win with his or her position. This style is appropriate in situations requiring an emergency decision, where there is no other option and someone must be willing to take the tough stand, or

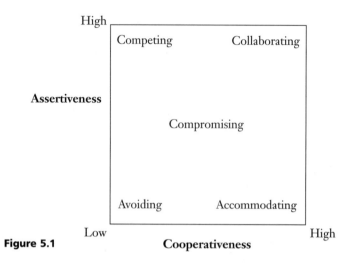

High

Competing   Collaborating

Assertiveness

Compromising

Avoiding   Accommodating

Low   High

Figure 5.1   **Cooperativeness**

where self-protection is essential. The downside of this style is that it intimidates others to the point where problems or important information may go underground and develop into unpredictable perceptions and actions that continue or escalate the conflict.

Accommodating. Behavior is based on giving up one's own interests in order to satisfy the other party's interests. A choice is made to yield. This style is appropriate when an issue is not of great importance to you and harmony is, or when the other party has all the power. The downside of this style is that if used excessively, neither you nor others have an opportunity to understand your real strength, and you may not know the satisfaction of having your interests fulfilled.

Avoiding. Behavior in which there is no attempt to satisfy either one's own or the other party's interests. A choice is made to remain apart from interactive engagement on the issue. This style is appropriate when the issue is of no importance to you or when used as a short-term strategy to buy time for thinking or for "cooling down," or, as with Accommodating, if the other person has unyielding power over you. The downside is that issues may persist and remain unresolved.

Compromising. Behavior in which each party sacrifices some of his or her own interests in order to satisfy some of the interests of the other. Each person negotiates to win some personal interests in exchange for yielding others. This style is useful when the issue is of some importance but there is not sufficient time or energy for a full-fledged collaborative process or when people have equal strength but are committed to mutually exclusive goals. It is also a fallback process when collaboration clearly is not going to produce a fully win/win solution. The downside of this style is that there may be missed opportunity for a more creative solution that would increase resources, productivity, and satisfaction.

Collaborating. Behavior that seeks a way to satisfy fully both parties' interests—a win/win solution. Each person examines issues important to both people and commits to exploration of alternative resolutions that address all concerns. This style is appropriate when both parties are committed to finding a mutual solution and have the time and energy to undertake the process. The downside is that the process may involve more time than is available or is appropriate for minor issues.

While research is limited on the styles used by various types to handle conflict, there is some evidence that the various types have a different initial reflex response to conflict. Note that in figure 5.2 the dichotomies of Extraversion–Introversion, Thinking–Feeling, and Judging–Perceiving seem to have the greatest impact on style with no statistically significant influence indicated in these studies by the Sensing–Intuition pair (Percival, Smitheram, and Kelly 1992; Johnson 1997).

Competing ETJ (males)	Collaborating EFJ
	Compromising ETJ (females) ITP* ETP
Avoiding ITJ IFP IFJ	Accommodating EFP

Both the findings of Percival et al and Johnson indicated that Compromising and Avoiding are the top two preferred styles for ITPs. However, Johnson's study indicated a slight preference for Avoiding which places them with all other Introverted types.

Figure 5.2

It is not surprising that Extraversion seems to influence a bias toward interactive styles. The mental energy of Extraversion seeks connection with the outer world. Add Thinking in its extraverted form, and ETJ types are usually able, as Myers has pointed out, "to organize facts and ideas into a logical sequence that states the subject, makes the necessary points, comes to a conclusion, and stops there without repetition" (Myers 1995, 68), a natural setup to select the competing style.

Managing conflict with collaboration or compromise requires a good deal of discussion, an activity welcomed by EFJ types in their quest to seek harmony between themselves and others. As interactive problem solving has become the "norm" for females in North America, perhaps this influences female ETJ types also to engage in the give and take of reaching a compromise at a level significantly greater than their fellow ETJs who happen to be male. Interestingly, the ETJs and EFJs will in theory both win their positions with the choices of competing and collaborating. The EFJs seem to seek to have the other party win as well.

That three of the Introverted types report a preference for Avoiding also reflects type theory. Introverts have reported in workshops that there are several reasons they retreat to their inner world when conflict occurs. Some report that they are actively processing information internally and are not yet in a position to suggest a solution. Their intent is ultimately to reveal or apply their solution. If another solution has been implemented before they reveal theirs, then all is well if the solution does not have a negative impact on them. If it does, they may then implement the solution they independently determined for themselves, sometimes unaware of how this may affect other people. Other Introverts report that dealing interactively with the emotion present in a conflict is difficult and seems out of control, so they retreat to the inner world that they can control to sort this out or to find a neutral place where they can work on the "real" issues, without the distraction of others' emotions. Psychologist Allen Hammer conjectures that "some Introverts . . . analyze a situation and conclude that more would be gained in terms of accomplishing a task by avoiding the conflict and focusing on the objective steps of the task than by processing or confronting" (Hammer 1996, 85).

It is curious perhaps that the ITPs and ETPs chose Compromising. Perhaps both types enjoy a good debate and do not typically see any solutions reached as affecting them personally in the way that Feeling types might. Debating with the other person may offer additional information or possibilities to the situation. Giving up some of their original position may be a small price to pay for this gain.

While it is helpful to understand what an initial reaction to a conflict might be for groups of a particular type, experience shows that individuals who combine a knowledge of type with an understanding of effective conflict management approaches go beyond a reflexive inclination and exercise choice as to how they work with the conflict. Knowledge and awareness support the ability to choose rather than react.

SECTION TWO

Great discoveries and
improvements invariably
involve the cooperation of
many minds.

Alexander Graham Bell

PUTTING KNOWLEDGE INTO PRACTICE

O kay, so now what?" you may be saying. I have all this information on the different types. I might even recognize my own type with its inherent strengths and weaknesses in conflict situations. This may be useful when I'm trying to resolve conflict with a partner whose type I know or with a team whose members have shared their types. But how am I supposed to figure out someone's type on the spot—or should I?

The final chapters of this book deal with the practice of applying type understanding to conflict management. It is not necessary, however, for one to be a type expert to use the steps toward conflict resolution recommended here. Likewise, it is not necessary to know the types of others in a conflict. The important thing is to recognize that people are different and may react to conflict in different ways. In the case of type, as with so many other things, knowledge gives us choice. Insight of type allows us to:

☐ Understand some fundamental ways people are different and react to conflict in different ways

☐ Be aware of how our own type has an impact on our reaction to conflict, the strengths of this natural approach, and where it is wise to broaden our response

☐ Recognize some clues as to how the other person may naturally react to conflict

☐ See the wisdom of including all four functions of Sensing, Intuition, Thinking, and Feeling in managing conflicts and understand some ways to see that all these functions are included

Today many people do, in fact, know their types and the types of people they live and work with. Honoring how your preferences function, as well as those opposite yours, makes conscious adapting and merging of mental processes easier. Use the kind of information provided in chapter 3 as a guidelines for working collaboratively with other people.

When one does not know the type of the other person but does understand the four functions, it's possible to listen for cues as to which functions seem to be expressed more by the other person, regardless of whether or not those are his or her actual preferences. Does the person want to see more details in order to get excited about your idea? Is a big picture perspective needed for the other person to make sense of what you are saying? If you begin talking logical consequences of options, does the other person communicate with you better? Does the other person continue to question how something is likely to have an impact on people personally?

The key word here is "listen." Most of us tend to listen for an opportunity to interject our own perspectives rather than ask questions to understand the perspectives of others.

We also can ask questions directly, such as "What do you need more of in our discussion—detailed specifics or a bigger picture perspective?" or "Do you need some time to reflect on what we've discussed so far, or would you rather continue talking it out now?"

The seven-step collaborative model described in chapter 6 can be followed by the person who knows type without using the labels of type. This involves first being aware of one's own type-based inclinations and using awareness of the contribution of all four functions and then intentionally seeing that all are included in generating and evaluating solution options. Or the model can be used by someone who does not know type but is open to exploring, understanding, and respecting differences among people.

Resolving conflict is rarely
about who is right. It is
about acknowledgment and
appreciation of differences.

Thomas Crum
The Magic of Conflict

A MODEL FOR RESOLVING CONFLICT
COLLABORATIVELY WITH TYPE

While all styles for handling conflict can be appropriate depending on the situation, collaboration is the style of choice when all stakeholders have both the time and inclination to reach a truly win/win solution and the significance of the conflict warrants this investment. Collaboration also can be the most difficult approach to undertake, as it requires patience and a commitment to an open mind for exploratory problem solving. Both of these may be in short supply in the midst of conflict! (See Appendix B for ways stress inherent in conflict can alter behavior for the different types.) Fortunately, users of type have an advantage. They recognize that use of different perspectives increases the potential for finding an effective solution. They also appreciate the process of collaboration as an opportunity for building or enhancing the skills that come with developing the less conscious aspects of our minds.

What follows is a seven-step process for incorporating type into a collaborative model. Included in this model is the opportunity to identify and disentangle the type-related issues from other problems. With this accomplished, and if the level of trust between the parties is high, then working through other issues can be achieved with more mutual understanding and respect. I am a fan of Roger Fisher and William Ury's seminal work on managing conflict, particularly as presented in the books, *Getting to Yes* (Fisher and Ury 1991) and *Getting Past No* (Ury 1993). Fisher and Ury advanced enormously the process of conflict management by outlining a process of negotiation on the basis of underlying interests rather than positions. Readers familiar with these volumes will recognize significant aspects of their ideas integrated with type in the seven-step model presented in this chapter. I highly recommend their books for clever, comprehensive, and effective strategies for use throughout the twists and turns of dealing with conflict.

Summary of the Seven Steps

1. A precondition for success: Intentionally move to a nondefensive attitude of openness with the intent to explore and learn rather than to defend a particular position.

2. Listen to each other's current positions, with each person putting himself or herself in the other's shoes for the moment and restating the other's position as it is heard.

3. Temporarily suspend each position and state the problem in terms of the interests and needs underlying these positions.

4. Identify areas of commonality in the two sets of interests and needs.

5. Identify areas of differences in the two sets of interests and needs and explore where type preferences may influence the differences.

6. Generate as many potential solutions as possible that will accommodate both sets of needs (including type differences). Review the options to see if type preferences have been accommodated. Discuss and jointly rank the options in order of priority.

7. Devise a plan for implementation (write it down!) and evaluation (set a follow-up date!).

STEP 1: *A precondition for success: Intentionally move to a nondefensive attitude of openness with the intent to explore and learn rather than to defend a particular position.*

This first step is typically the most difficult in the entire process of conflict management. It is also a step on which the likelihood of successful resolution depends. Many people stress that the first step is to define the problem. In my experience, this may be very difficult due to the influence of our hard wiring. Type suggests that people of different types may define the problem quite differently. Remember Sue with the late reports? (See chapter 2.) Sensing with its focus on specific events may see the problem as getting Sue to turn in certain reports on time. Intuition with its focus on themes may see the problem as Sue's general chronic procrastination. With type differences such as these, a conflict can escalate from two people attempting in good faith simply to define the problem.

Push a Different Button

Rather than trying to define the problem when a disagreement begins, I propose you push a different button. Ever see those old-fashioned switches you punched to make the lights work? When you pushed the "ON" button, the "OFF" button popped out and vice versa. For all of us there are many issues on which we remain fairly open, neutral, and relaxed—our hot button remains off. Other issues, however, push our hot buttons on due to the hard wiring of our type or due to some other part of us we want to protect out of an underlying fear. In conflict the trick is to remember that we can control which button is pushed. We do this by taking physical or mental action.

The Physical Button

Our bodies, and the emotions they carry, provide a helpful first clue that there is a conflict. So developing general body awareness is a helpful strategic skill in conflict management. The time to take note is with awareness of the first emotional or physical tension since either is present for a valid reason. Something important to us is threatened—a value, principle, person, object, or belief. Responding to our fear, our autonomic nervous system kicks in with its protective impulse. From the hormonal rush, we involuntarily tighten our muscles in a fight/flight response. Perhaps our jaw, shoulders, or stomach tighten. There may be a tingling in our limbs as the blood rushes away from our vital organs to our limbs, a relic from the limited choice of fleeing or fighting available to our primeval ancestors. When we learn to isolate in our awareness that particular muscles are tense and then relax them, our mental attitude will also relax toward openness. Taking several deep breaths helps. These physical actions also move us into our introverted side, which happens to be the environment where this first step in conflict management is accomplished.

When a disagreement initially occurs, we may be unaware of these physical sensations and proceed as if the matter is being resolved smoothly. Indeed, if the matter is of little concern to us, we can do just that. Fortunately, if there is more to the dispute than there appeared at first, our body remains an ally and is perfectly willing to give us cues as the process proceeds. Staying aware of our physical and emotional responses throughout the problem-solving effort gives us access to the signals our body sends indicating whether we are on the path to explore and learn or whether we have moved to a position of defense. Pushing off the hot button is a management skill we can use at any time in the process in order to get back on track.

The Mental Button
We can also push a different button mentally. Just as we are hard wired for the involuntary fight/flight physical response, so are we hard wired for an automatic mental response influenced by our type. Conflict management generally requires that we temporarily, at least, suspend this response. In my experience, the process of pushing a different button occurs in two stages. The first step is to begin by being aware of and affirming our natural reaction before we speak it aloud. This is like saying to ourselves in an internal nonjudgmental way "of course! That's a natural reaction for my type." The second step is to recognize we have a choice: to protect out of fear or to open our minds to exploration. If we affirm without negative judgment that the first reaction is a valid and even predictable one, given one's type or past experience, it is easier to take the second step toward openness. Giving ourselves negative feedback about the natural reaction only adds an agenda of having to defend that understandable response to ourselves. This wastes time and energy that are better used to move toward resolution.

Like any management skill, this takes practice to become more automatic—even in the face of an emotional outburst from the other party.

Some self-statements like the following honor the natural inclinations of each type and can make it easier to push that different button.

ESTJ/ENTJ

The way I see this matter makes sense. Realistically, though, I'm not likely to get the cooperation I need to settle this matter if I don't take seriously the concerns of (other stakeholders, my partner, etc.)

ESFJ/ENFJ

I am sure I have a good solution. And at the same time, (the other person) may not feel validated if I don't take (his or her) perspective seriously. Perhaps (his or her) opinion says more about where (he or she) is than it does about me.

ESTP/ENTP

There is a dynamic process going on with this conflict that could produce an effective and interesting solution. I wonder what will come up if we continue to talk.

ESFP/ENFP

I wish there weren't a conflict here. At the same time, this could be an interesting adventure if I choose not to personalize the issues.

ISTJ/INTJ

I prefer to handle this problem myself and I would do it well. At the same time, I just might get some important data or an intriguing idea that would produce an even better solution if I hang in.

ISFJ/INFJ

I really prefer ignoring this conflict. At the same time, I can make this situation better if I choose not to personalize what (he or she) is saying and instead approach this conflict as a mutual problem.

ISTP/INTP

I don't really see the need for much discussion about this issue. At the same time, it could be useful or interesting to check out (his or her) thinking.

ISFP/INFP

I don't want to get involved in this conflict. At the same time, deep down I do want (the other person) to feel good about the situation.

Behind all of these suggestions for whole types is the attitude that says, "I can probably produce a better solution and learn something as well, if I am willing to explore." (For an extensive discussion of this attitude of mental openness in personal relationships, see *Do I Have to Give Up Me in Order to Be Loved by You* by Jordan Paul and Margaret Paul.)

If you're alert to type, you have probably become aware that this step involves accessing our introverted side. Note that the fleeing part of a fight/flight response is not the same thing. It may be just as difficult for introverts to move to a nondefensive position if they have retreated to their inner worlds as it is for Extraverts to reverse their outward-directed energies.

Once we have pushed the button for openness, we can move to the next step that clarifies assumptions, gives practice in the important skill of active listening, and builds trust with the other party, all essential components of collaborative problem solving.

STEP 2: *Listen to each other's current positions, with each person putting himself or herself in the other's shoes for the moment and restating the other's position as it is heard.*

People generally find it easier to stretch to other viewpoints once they feel they have been "heard" accurately, even if they know the other person disagrees. So it is crucial that each person be allowed to state his or her current position about the conflict, including any emotions that may have led to this position.

> Romero (ISTJ) announced to his wife, Margaret (ESFP) and their two children at dinner that he didn't think the family should plan to take their usual two-week vacation to the beach. There was too much going on at work for him to get away that long. Margaret got angry remembering that she had already adjusted her own work agenda to accommodate the vacation. Both husband and wife felt bad listening to the children's disappointed cries of "But Daddy, you promised!" With a major conflict brewing, Margaret and Romero agreed to talk further about it later that evening once the children were working on their homework.

The task of the speaker is to state his or her position as clearly and briefly as possible using a natural style of communication. The task of the listener is to move to and remain in the nondefensive position, with a view toward being able to restate the position back to the speaker. It is not the time to add personal input no matter how strongly it is felt. (Pushing the Off button reduces both the emotional and body tension that may re-ignite as the other position is heard.)

The listener then checks with the speaker to see if the position has been heard correctly. If the speaker does not yet feel the listener has heard accurately, he or she may clarify a point but not *add* a point. The speaker/listener roles are then reversed and the same procedure of listening, restating, and giving opportunity for clarification is followed.

The purpose of this step is to identify current positions—not to discuss and evaluate them. It is a good time to state felt emotions as well. Core positions are marked in bold face in this exchange between Romero and Margaret.

Romero: *As I said,* **I don't think we should take a long vacation this year. I just can't take the time off work. There's too much pressure to complete the department's project.**

Margaret: *So you don't think we should take a vacation this year because you have too much pressure at work to take the time off.*

Romero: *Let me clarify that I said we shouldn't take a* long *vacation this year—our usual two weeks. I wasn't saying we shouldn't take any vacation at all.*

Margaret: *So you don't think we should take a vacation as long as two weeks this year.*

Romero: *That's right.*

Margaret: **I'm really surprised and frustrated. Two weeks isn't very long for a vacation. We both work hard the rest of the year and deserve it. I think your job means more to you these days than your family does.**

Romero: *You're saying that you're surprised and frustrated because we work hard and deserve a two-week vacation. You also think my job means more to me than our family does.*

Margaret: *Yes.*

Their differing positions are now stated and satisfactorily clarified. Incidentally, people alert to type can often pick up the influence of preferences in this first step of stating positions. It's a skill that helps remove judgment as they listen to the position being stated and experience the body language of the person speaking. A summary of some of these effects are listed here. (See chapter 2 for a comprehensive description of these influences.

Summary of Type Influences for Stating Positions

Extraversion and Introversion
Body language, pacing, visible intensity, and external or internal processing. Extraverts tend to physically move about and increase their physical and verbal intensity until they believe their positions are understood. Introverts may pause more and restrain the use of body and words.

Sensing and Intuition
How the position is stated and what information is included. A Sensing preference often uses many facts of "who, what, when, where" specificity. Intuition is likely to include meaning or intent.

Thinking and Feeling
Value differences of logic- versus person-centered concerns. Note Romero's focus on objective tasks (Thinking) and Margaret's on the impact on people (Feeling). There also may be personal or accusatory elements related to the negative expression of these functions.

Judging and Perceiving
Relates to a desire to bring about closure or to keep options open. From a Judging preference it can sound as if the discussion is over, while it can seem as if a person with a preference for Perceiving is not genuinely engaged in problem solving.

In spite of an understanding and acceptance of these type differences intellectually, people generally still feel annoyed or worse as they listen to the other's position. It is a good time to practice the difficult skill of keeping the hot button off. The process is proceeding, and step 3 brings some relief!

STEP 3: *Temporarily suspend each position and state the problem in terms of the interests and needs underlying these positions.*

The ultimate objective of conflict is to satisfy some underlying interests and needs. Step 3 is where these are identified. Again, the awareness and acceptance of type differences helps each person to stay in an open position of exploration rather than get stuck in an attitude of protection.

This step forces the parties to deal with significant issues directly instead of indirectly, an interpersonal dynamic that leads to increased trust. Defining the problem from the standpoint of underlying interests and needs produces more fundamental problem definition than is likely to occur earlier in the process when people are still defending their positions.

> Underlying Romero's position that the family should forgo their two-week beach vacation is part of his solution for handling a serious concern. His company is restructuring and he sees a possible job loss in his future. He's worried there won't be enough money for essentials, let alone vacations. This possibility is something he hasn't wanted to share with his wife and children unless and until it happens.
>
> Margaret's position that they've always gone away for two weeks and this year should be no different stems from her interest in having the family enjoy time together without the distractions of work, school, and community activities. Their argument has centered on their opposing positions with no progress toward resolution. Romero's indirect justification for support of his position ("I can't take the time from work this year.") has escalated the argument because Margaret assumes he cares more for work than for his family.
>
> If they dare to deal with the underlying issues, they are more likely to find a creative solution which accommodates both

realities—they may have less money and they would like to spend uninterrupted time together.

For this step I find it very useful for the two parties actually to sit or stand side by side with paper to write on—which has a line drawn down the middle designating a side to each participant. Each person lists, on his or her side, individual interests or needs that have led to the stated position, without re-stating the position or suggesting another solution. At this point neither party evaluates nor judges any of the interests or needs. All are respected as being important to the person stating them.

This is not a time to be shy about the interests. Romero and Margaret generated the following list interactively.

Romero

☐ May lose my job and want us to have a financial cushion.
☐ Don't want to reduce our savings any more than necessary.
☐ Believe part of my job as husband and father is to be a good provider.
☐ Don't want you and the children to have to give up our way of life. Saving cost of a 2-week vacation will help maintain this.
☐ Keep spending under control.
☐ Don't feel like playing when I'm this worried.
☐ Want my boss to see me as hardworking and indispensable.
☐ Share valuable family time together.
  (Reminded of this when he heard Margaret's interests)

Margaret

☐ Vacation is quality time with each other which balances our hard work with play.
☐ Need to support each other more than ever in difficult times.
☐ Want to keep life as normal as possible for the children.
☐ All of us need to relax.
☐ Play helps reduce tension and get our minds off worry.
☐ Want family to have priority over all other things.
☐ Have enough money to pay the basic bills in a difficult time.
  (Reminded of this when she heard Romero's interests)

Type differences as well as content have an impact on process at this stage. Extraverts typically delve deeper into the thinking process by talking aloud, bouncing one idea off another. Introverts, on the other hand, delve deeper into the thought process as they reflect. Accommodation should be made for time talking together as well as time reflecting individually to identify these underlying factors.

For both Thinking and Feeling types, it may take additional time to identify interests and needs stemming from Feeling values. It is often easier to tease out the logical reasons inherent in a position than it is the person-centered values. Again, the body and emotions can be an ally. A lingering sensation of discomfort or confusion is a cue to ask for more time. ("I don't know why yet, but something doesn't feel right. I'd like a little more time to think about this.")

Then with all known underlying interests and needs stated, it is time to begin finding a solution to the conflict.

STEP 4: *Identify areas of commonality in the two sets of interests and needs.*

This is the breakthrough step, as the process now becomes one of mutual problem solving. Invariably, there are individual interests or needs not held by the other person. In most cases, participants are surprised at how many interests they share, and there is a noticeable shift to positive energy and momentum as these are discovered.

> Romero and Margaret quickly agreed that saving money was a significant concern in order to cover the possibility that Romero would lose his job. It was also easy for Margaret to understand that Romero shared her concern for family time once they were dealing with underlying issues rather than opposing positions.

People skilled with type also recognize that differences of preference may mask a shared interest or need by emphasizing a different aspect of the same thing.

> Romero, with preferences for Introversion, Sensing, Thinking, and Judging (ISTJ) listed as one of his underlying interests that he wanted to keep the family strong by planning for contingencies so that basic essentials could be met if he was between jobs.
>
> Margaret with preferences for Extraversion, Sensing,

Feeling, and Perception (ESFP) listed a need for the family to be strengthened through shared experiences of play.

Not only could Margaret and Romero pick up the common concern for strengthening the family, but also each had to access and thus strengthen the less preferred sides of their personalities when they acknowledged the importance of both fiscal security and relationship building.

Therefore, effective use of type knowledge increases the ability for us to stretch and use the opposites of our preferences to see past differences to areas of commonality. The conflict management process then becomes a catalyst for type development. Paraphrasing what Myers is reported to have said, we don't have to conjure up situations to increase type development—life is one big laboratory! (McCaulley 1987)

STEP 5: *Identify areas of differences in the two sets of interests and needs and explore where type preferences may influence the differences.*

Noting the inevitable differences in interests and needs without evaluating them is a respect for and an honoring of legitimate differences. Without premature judgment, differences are likely to become manageable. Many of these are type related. By verbally acknowledging how type preferences may be influencing differences, the dissimilarities often seem less abrasive. And if we recognize that the best solution to a problem usually involves all the preferences, we increase the possibility that the best solution will develop.

Margaret was reminded that providing financial security and stability is one way a person preferring STJ demonstrates love.

Romero appreciated Margaret's natural SFP focus on building loving relationships through time spent together.

Discussion in this step also sorts out what may seem like a type issue but, in fact, may be something else. For example, Romero's concern to complete tasks at work without a break was due to fear of loss of his job, not just because he has a preference for Judging. Potential loss of a job was a major concern to Romero and became a concern to Margaret as a result of their working through step 3. They differed, however, on ways to *meet* the challenge.

> **STEP 6:** *Generate as many potential solutions as possible that will accommodate both sets of needs (including type differences). Review the options to see if type preferences have been accommodated. Discuss and jointly rank the options in order of priority.*

This is a time to think, "more is better." It is also a time to think creatively. Taming wild ideas is far easier than drawing out the banal!

> Romero and Margaret produced a number of possible solutions that would accommodate both the need for fiscal restraint and shared family experiences without outside distractions. They found themselves laughing at the inadvisability of some of them (e.g., embezzling money to finance a trip) and intrigued with the promise of others (e.g., looking for a way to barter something for the use of a friend's beach house).

Some types find this step more engaging than do others. Extraverts typically enjoy processing aloud and broaden their thinking as they hear other ideas and information. Introverts typically do their best thinking internally and find brainstorming a hindrance. When Introverts are involved, it is generally advisable to conduct this step over several sessions.

Another challenge to type differences is the need to resist the inclination to judge options prematurely. Sensing types will find some options not practical or not sufficiently proven; Intuition types will tend to reject solutions that seem limiting; Thinking types will find some options too illogical; Feeling types will consider some too hardhearted.

Assuming that the best solutions incorporate all four preferences of Sensing, Intuition, Thinking, and Feeling, it is also important to make sure proposed solutions accommodate any preferences not represented by the participating parties' types. Refer to chapter 1 for some suggestions on how to accomplish this.

> It was when Romero and Margaret realized that neither had a natural preference for Intuition that it occurred to them to

involve the children in the discussion. Sure enough, out of the kids' additional ideas came their ultimate family decision to spend a week exploring the "vacation" spots close to home—the ones they were always too busy to discover.

Ranking the priorities involves rooting out the options regarded by both parties as frivolous or that defy legal, ethical, or religious boundaries and then negotiating the remainder with focus on a win/win solution.

A place to begin is to return to the interests and needs that are mutually shared. These may form part of the solution or establish part of the criteria for a satisfactory solution.

> Romero and Margaret shared interests in spending less money in their current situation and reaching a solution that would reduce, not increase, stress.

Negotiating the remainder of the options is one of the best opportunities for type development possible. Using techniques such as putting yourself in the other person's place to understand where they are coming from is an opportunity to view the conflict from another perspective. For example, a Feeling type can gain some objective distance by temporarily stepping outside the natural boundaries of how his or her own values will be affected. A Thinking type can become aware in a more personal way of how a decision is affecting others. From these temporary identities, discuss the pros and cons and logical consequences of each option, incorporating both the Thinking criteria of objective data and the Feeling criteria of likely impact on people.

Consider ranking options separately and then comparing the rankings. This may help narrow the field if you take both your top ranked options and find ways to merge them.

> Romero and Margaret and the children merged his top-ranked option of setting a firm modest limit on what could be spent with her top option of taking several weekend trips and elected to spend two nights in a downtown hotel while they explored attractions in a nearby city. They also set aside four weekend days for day trips spread throughout the summer.

When there are non-negotiable interests reflected in an option, you may have to agree to disagree and seek a compromise. In this case, look for ways to barter interests. ("What can you give me if I give you this?") On the other hand, if you step into the other person's skin, what seemed rigidly unchangeable may seem less so when viewed from another perspective. Fisher and Ury (1991) recommend that you think about what you will do if the negotiation is not successful. Considering what specifically you will do may alter your perspective on what is truly non-negotiable so that additional options seem attractive.

> Margaret did indeed enter the first evening's conflict management discussions determined to take the children and go to the beach whether her husband joined them or not. When she realized her back-up plan would need to be funded solely from her own income, she felt much more open about considering other options.

Using a variation of the game of listening to the angel and devil sitting separately on each shoulder, give voice to your mental functions in the same way. Try putting your Sensing function on one shoulder and Intuitive function on the other and ask what each needs or wants in this situation. Then do the same exercise with Thinking and Feeling. Not only will you likely gain new perspective, but it's yet another type development opportunity! Try referring to chapter 1 if the voices need some prompting.

The points made here are some intentional ways to incorporate type. Type will continue to influence the process in other ways through this negotiation stage, and it is useful to be alert to some of the differences described next.

☐ Extraverts will more likely talk out the negotiating while Introverts will want time to think it through.

☐ The person preferring Sensing will want to stay focused on the point under discussion and will likely be annoyed if the Intuition preference takes the other person into tangential thoughts. When the person preferring Intuition presents underlying interests or needs not mentioned in earlier discussions or lists, it is a good idea to add these options to the mix *and* to see if additional ones might be suggested. However, a "thank you" to the Sensing person is in order if this happens—expanding options at this point in the process is a challenge to the natural inclination of Sensing.

☐ Someone with a preference for Thinking is likely to look for a principle that can be applied to any number of similar situations. A Feeling type will want to be more situation specific. Feeling types also like decisions made by consensus and generally have more patience with the longer discussions required to satisfy all parties. It may prove to be false economy of time and effort to sacrifice a long-term goal of commitment to a shorter-term goal of deciding quickly if the solution somehow conflicts with a value held dear by the person with a preference for Feeling. The difficulty is that the Feeling type is not always aware immediately how the solution is in conflict. Often though, the Feeling person will have a sense of uneasiness, suggesting it may be wise to ask for more time in order to figure out the source of the uneasiness.

☐ When negotiating with someone with a preference for Perceiving, recognize the natural inclination is to keep options open as long as possible unless that person has already made a firm decision. It probably does not mean that they are not interested in reaching a resolution. Realize, too, that the energy of the Judging attitude is directed toward reaching a decision, and a person with this preference may be struggling to reverse the direction from deciding to exploring. When negotiating with someone with a preference for Judging, it is especially helpful to find points where agreement can be reached and to develop drafts of *potential* solutions whenever possible. The task of the Judging type is to accept these as potential rather than final.

STEP 7: *Devise a plan for implementation (write it down!) and evaluation (set a follow-up date!).*

Devising and writing down a plan of implementation that includes a follow-up date for evaluation serves several purposes. It increases the likelihood that a decision, so carefully made, will be carried out by clarifying who will do what by when. It also includes an opportunity to determine how effectively the selected solution met all the underlying interests and concerns identified earlier.

When deciding who will take on what responsibility, allow for the accommodation of type differences, recognizing that most often people select tasks that primarily involve their natural preferences. On the other hand, someone aware of wanting to develop his or her "opposites" may choose a task that will help develop the skills of these less-developed functions.

Wisely, the parties will commit to meet a mutually determined goal and deadline. Wisely, they also allow flexibility for how the goals and deadline are met. The Judging and Perceiving preferences differ greatly in how they approach a deadline. See chapter 1 for a reminder of these differences.

Happily, Romero and Margaret's family decided after their week of vacationing at home, that they would like to repeat that experience more often—perhaps renting canoes, biking, hiking, and picnicking in unexplored spots on a weekend day scattered throughout the year. They agreed to rotate responsibilities for making arrangements and selecting spots, deciding they really worked well together as a team.

Additional Ideas for Teams or Organizations

The steps and examples described in this chapter have been written with a focus on managing conflict between two individuals. Quite often conflict must be negotiated between groups of people—labor and management, students and faculty, citizens and government, or department and department. The seven-step model still can be followed with most of the steps occurring twice: first within each group individually and then between the representatives selected to negotiate on behalf of each group. (If individuals disagree with another within their own group significantly enough to produce anger, it is a good idea to settle such differences before going into the primary negotiation process with another group.)

Between each step, the representatives select occasions to return to their respective groups and work with them through the appropriate tasks, such as clearly grasping the other side's initial position; identifying underlying interests and needs, commonalities, differences; generating options; or for developing a plan of implementation and evaluation. In the case of ranking the options for resolution that were generated, each group is wise to negotiate a ranking within their group so their representatives know their latitude for bargaining.

If the negotiating representative is actually a team, odds are that the team members collectively will not represent all the functions as natural preferences, anymore than an individual does. Therefore, designating specific team members to be advocates for the missing preferences better ensures that all mental functions will be included in resolutions reached.

Using the Model with Mediation

The seven steps can also be followed in the process of mediation, with the mediator guiding the participants through the process, and keeping them focused along the way. If the participating parties are familiar with and respect type, the mediator can assist by pointing out possible expressions of the preferences, particularly when the expression is both clearly type-related and is somehow resisted by the other party. Like anything else, however, the use of type is both a science and an art. Artistic use suggests pointing out this awareness sparingly, when it is clearly needed to facilitate the process. Otherwise the first agreement reached may be that the mediator is a hindrance!

When participants other than the mediator are unfamiliar with type, the mediator can use awareness of type without the labels of type to elicit the contributions of and accommodate the needs of each preference. Here are some examples:

☐ Would either of you like more "face" time? More time for reflection? (Extraversion–Introversion)

☐ Is there any additional information either of you need? (Sensing)

☐ If you *were* to consider additional options, what might they be? (Intuition)

☐ Is there another strategy that might attain the same results? (Thinking)

☐ What do you value most about your desired outcome? (Feeling)

☐ What would it take for you to reach a decision? (Judging)

☐ What would it take for you to consider additional options? (Perceiving)

The Quick Reference guides found in chapter 2 provide concise material for framing such questions. One question that engages a previously neglected preference can often open a blocked negotiation process.

A blunder at the right
moment is better than
cleverness at the wrong
time.

Carolyn Wells,
children's author

WHEN IS TYPE APPROPRIATE TO USE IN CONFLICT RESOLUTION?

type can be a powerful resource when used appropriately in managing conflict. It can also exacerbate a conflict if used inappropriately.

Levels of Conflict

If left unresolved, conflicts can proceed through several levels, from a simple misunderstanding to outright annihilation. Resolution is best achieved at the early stages; it may be impossible at the highest levels.

Level One: *A Misunderstanding*

Some would say this is not yet a conflict. Mathematician John Nash referred to this as "haggling" as opposed to conflict (Nash 1996). Typically, clarifying assumptions or needs prevents a confrontation from occurring. With regard to type, often only one or two functions are being articulated while the other party's mind is more easily engaged with other preferences. For example, a Thinking type neglects to offer appreciation before critiquing the work of a Feeling type and the Feeling type can't integrate the critique. An Intuitive needs a larger context to understand an immediate task assigned by a Sensing boss.

While it would be nice if we were all vigilantly alert to the type needs of each other, the reality is that in the busyness of life, we most often communicate and behave out of our own needs. The responsibility is our own, therefore, to speak up for what we need. Type understanding gives us the language for doing much of this. ("I want to hear your critique, but I can hear it better if you will first let me know what you think is good about my work" or "Can you help me understand the big picture of which this task is a part?")

Level Two: *Problem-Solving Mode*

At this level, there is a disagreement over goals, needs, values, or process. The problem, not the person, becomes the focus of discussion. No one is personally attacked. The situation becomes one of mutual respect and openness to exploration for the best solution. A collaborative process of conflict management is possible and type can be used as outlined in the seven-step model.

Level Three: *Protective Mode*

Now the problem is personalized; an internal conflict has been triggered. Solving the stated problem takes a backseat to protecting some part of a person that is vulnerable—quite often unconsciously so. People cling to a stated position from which they cannot move. There is little openness and little risk taking. People at this level may or may not engage with others even to pretend resolution is under way. More likely if they engage at all it is with a pseudo problem-solving process. Persons may exhibit passive-aggressive or controlling behavior or inappropriate compliance. At this stage, trying to connect with a person using the language of type is probably counter-productive. The issue is more likely one of the heart not the head.

On the other hand, if a person learns to recognize the physical and emotional tension that alerts to operating at this level, that individual can also learn to move to a position of openness and exploration and eventually "ratchet down" to a problem-solving level.

Level Four: *Competitive Mode*

At this level, people have developed a win/lose mentality and they want to make sure they are the winner. Mutual problem solving is not possible as there is no concern for others' interests—only their own. When dealing with a person operating at this level, you can make the situation explicit and ask, "Have you decided this is a win/lose situation?" If the answer is "no," then ask what it would take for him or her to be able to collaborate rather than compete with you. If the answer is "yes," your only choice may be to join the battle or, alternatively, cut your losses and let the other person win, particularly if he or she holds power over you.

Level Five: *Revenge Mode*
The intent is now to destroy the other party and the battle becomes more important than what the fight is supposed to be about. Third-party intervention generally is useless except to separate the warring sides or to render one side powerless. Safety is the critical issue. Civil and international wars reach this stage—as do, unfortunately, individuals. The film, *The War of the Roses* (CBS 1991) is a dark-humor portrayal of a couple that ends their conflict tragically at this level.

Appropriate use of type between conflicting parties occurs at the first and second levels. At the third level, individuals can get themselves back on track to a problem-solving level. If the parties are at different levels, but within the first three, then awareness of type can help them get to the same stage. The use of active listening by paraphrasing back what was heard from the other (going with their flow), followed by a statement of your own need or perspective, will help accomplish this at the first two levels. For example, "I think you're telling me that you need me to be less dogmatic when I make our group's presentation to the director. Give me a minute to see how I can rephrase our position."

Other Appropriate Uses of Type
Following are examples of situations where it is appropriate to use psychological type in dealing with conflicts.

When type is influencing the source of the conflict.
Example: One party with a preference for Sensing keeps bringing the focus of discussion back to a solution that has demonstrated evidence of success and the other person with a preference for Intuition insists on trying something with unproven potential.

When type differences are affecting the process of conflict resolution.
Example: An Extravert gets frustrated with the reflective silence of an Introvert and decides the introvert is not involved.

When type can help point out blind spots in the problem-solving process.
Example: A Thinking type is not vocalizing concern for the impact on people, or a Feeling type is unable to hear the interests of the other party because these interests conflict with a personal value.

When the behavioral inclination in type preferences can help transcend cultural differences so that some commonality can be acknowledged between disagreeing parties across cultural or gender lines.
Example: Traditional gender patterns in a work or personal relationship may mean an assertive ENTJ woman is always expected to play a subordinate role. While understanding that regardless of gender, an ENTJ's inclination is to take charge and lead may not change the cultural realities, this knowledge of type can open the door for negotiating some opportunities for leadership for this woman within the context of a particular setting. Since working from strengths produces better results, productive outcomes can gradually help relax rigid customs that constrain people's natural talents.

Possible Inappropriate Uses of Type
The following situations raise at least a cautionary warning about overt use of type in managing conflict.

When one party believes that type can solve virtually all problems.
Example: One clue that this may be the case is when all issues seem to be explained by type and there is resistance to consider other possibilities.

When type is viewed by any party as a static pigeonholing rather than a dynamic process offering conscious choices.
Example: A clue may be when someone describes type as "causing" certain behaviors. For example, "You're just saying that because you're an ISTP" or "We can't let you head that project because as an ENFP you won't be organized enough." This is an inaccurate and unethical use of type. Rather than engage in this kind of dialogue, a good question to ask is, "What would we have to change in order to resolve this issue?"

When talking type differences becomes a way of intellectualizing to the exclusion of acknowledging and validating the feelings experienced by the parties in the conflict.

Example: Emotions are always involved in a conflict, even when the demeanor of the participants is calm. Treat them as a fact of life. To ignore these feelings is to invite them to worsen, detracting from, and most likely preventing, effective resolution. If feelings are intense, it might be wise to allow some passage of time before attempting to solve the problem. This may be particularly true for Feeling types who need time to gain objectivity through engagement of their Thinking function.

Recognizing your own emotions and acknowledging that they are present for a reason is important even if not yet fully understood by yourself or the other party. To invite the other party to do so is an important skill in conflict management that can actually help the process proceed in a more timely fashion. ("I feel very frustrated about the lack of recognition for my group's efforts on that last project. My team is not motivated to take on this new assignment." Or "I'm really hurt and fearful when you won't talk to me about that broken promise. I'm wondering what you're feeling.")

Acknowledging and legitimizing feelings early in the process often defuses the developing tension to the point where the conflict dissipates. Validating someone's importance is often the unspoken agenda disguised as some other issue. This is important for all types, and particularly so for Feeling types. Thinking types generally are aware of wanting their *ideas* validated as having merit, but they may be less aware of wanting their *feelings* validated.

With a discussion of feelings present in the situation, an important agenda item is taken care of, and problem solving can proceed more effectively.

Clearly Inappropriate Use of Type

Type is not appropriate and may complicate conflict resolution if one party wants to talk type implications and the other does not or if the other party does not know anything about type. Either situation may be a good time for the party interested in type to do one or both of the following: talk the concepts of type without the type nomenclature (see chapter 6, page 80) and/or be willing to explore other factors that may be imbedded in the conflict.

I dogmatise and I am
contradicted, and in this
conflict of opinions and
sentiments I find delight.

Samuel Johnson

EPILOGUE

So there you have it—the contradictory differences in our minds actually support creative solutions to problems and disputes. This book has explained some of the reasons why we fight based on these differences and provided tools for how we can use this knowledge strategically to win—together. Introduced early in the process of managing conflict, use of type can help prevent the differences from escalating to a level where resolution becomes impossible.

Conflict is a daily fact of life. Therefore, with each dispute we have unending opportunity in this laboratory called life to grow and develop into fuller, more capable human beings. The issues may involve contractual negotiations or a teenager's curfew, arrangement of office space or settling territorial rights, contesting a repair bill or negotiating a trade agreement. There may be time to develop a well-crafted solution or we may have to deal with unexpected occurrences in the urgency of the moment. The fact is that in most of our daily conflicts, knowledge and awareness honed with ongoing practice are the tools that give us the freedom to make the choice for creative resolution. When we find ourselves stressed or indecisive, engaging all four mental functions of Sensing, Intuition, Thinking, and Feeling separately and intentionally helps us develop the habit of solving our minor conflicts before they take on major status. When others attack or have emotional outbursts, we can go with their flow, take on an attitude of curiosity and sense of mental adventure, and join with them to become mutual problem solvers. We can seek to understand their positions even if they don't initially show interest in ours. And we can start or adapt our communication to the language of their minds.

The investment in this skill-building endeavor pays off in more creative resolutions to life's complex and less complicated problems; and with increased trust, respect, and freedom in our relationships—both with others and within ourselves.

> *"It turns out that the resolution of conflict and the discovery of a better way of being, working, and living in the world occur simultaneously."*
>
> —Kenneth Cloke and Joan Goldsmith
> *Resolving Conflict at Work*

> *"God is the name by which I designate all things which cross my willful path violently and recklessly, all things which upset my subjective views, plans, and intentions, and change the course of my life for better or worse."*
>
> —Carl Jung

APPENDIX: EXAMPLE OF NEGOTIATION IN A BUSINESS SETTING USING THE SEVEN-STEP MODEL

Source of the conflict: Disagreement over whether to institute a personnel policy allowing telecommuting.

Scenario: Several employees have been requesting that their organization experiment with the practice of telecommuting. The ESTJ manager has thus far consistently opposed the idea. Following a company training session on conflict management, the affected employees have decided to try again and have appointed an ENFP in their group to serve as their spokesperson and negotiator.

> **ENFP:** *I'd like to talk further about the proposal that we institute an option for our staff to telecommute.*

> **ESTJ:** *As I've said before, it's a nice idea on paper but it won't work—it's too difficult to supervise. Keeping up with time spent on which project is already tedious. And without ongoing contact you lose track of weekly, let alone daily, productivity.*

ENFP: *You're missing the point. It's ludicrous not to allow, even encourage, telecommuting, given both family needs today and environmental concerns in an area already choked with daily traffic.*

ESTJ: *Family concerns are all well and good, but overhead costs are already up 14 percent over budget this year and cost overruns on projects are 10 percent higher than projections. We can't afford to risk nonproductive time for salaried personnel.*

ENFP: *And I believe we'll have higher productivity by keeping morale high and by being able to hire committed, hardworking young adults who won't have to make as many choices between family and work. You're insisting on micromanagement, and as a result we're not going to attract the best and brightest. Highly creative people don't like to be micromanaged.*

STEP 1: *A precondition for success: Intentionally move to a nondefensive attitude of openness with the intent to explore and learn rather than to defend a particular position.*

ESTJ: *OK, OK. You pushed a hot button with that micromanagement charge. It's obvious you're not going to let the issue go away if we don't get a decision made. So let's hash it out and get that decision made. (At this point, a deep breath helps the manager to assume an open attitude, a change that makes it easier for her employee to make the same shift. The manager then continues.)*

STEP 2: *Listen to each other's current positions, with each person putting himself or herself in the other's shoes for the moment and restating the other's position as it is heard.*

ESTJ: *(continuing) Let me see if I understand your position. You believe we'll be able to keep and hire highly productive people who want more flexibility to take care of family needs as they occur.*

ENFP: *That's right. And I gather you believe productivity will go down if there's no visible way to monitor it—and that is a concern, particularly at a time when costs are already over budget.*

STEP 3: *Temporarily suspend each position and state the problem in terms of the interests and needs underlying these positions.*

> **ESTJ:** *You got it. So if we use that human resources training from last month, let's suspend our positions for the moment and check out our underlying needs. Let's write them down. I'm concerned about:*
>
> > *Loss of customers from not meeting project deadlines*
> >
> > *Having to hire more personnel to meet those deadlines*
> >
> > *Keeping overhead costs down to increase profitability*
> >
> > *Minimizing paperwork—which seems to me will increase with record keeping of work time spread over twenty-four hours of an employee's day*

> **ENFP:** *I share your desire to minimize paperwork. I also feel like we're getting into positions again if we assume telecommuting does or doesn't involve more paperwork.*

> **ESTJ:** *Fair enough. What are your concerns?*

> **ENFP:** *Obviously, the bottom line of profitability.*
>
> > *And high productivity.*
> >
> > *Also, high morale.*
> >
> > *There's also the issue about lifestyles balanced between work and family.*
> >
> > *Availability for family needs and availability to work without worrying about the care a sick child is getting.*
> >
> > *And we have an environmental concern too—to put fewer cars on the road.*

STEP 4: *Identify areas of commonality in the two sets of interests and needs.*

> **ESTJ:** *Well, we certainly raise different issues. On which ones are we in agreement?*

> **ENFP:** *Certainly profitability, high productivity, and keeping*

customers. That last one was implicit for me with profitability. You've made the bottom-line need more explicit. That's helpful.

ESTJ: *And you've made the morale factor more explicit. I agree that's essential for long-term productivity and recruitment.*

STEP 5: *Identify areas of differences in the two sets of interests and needs and explore where type preferences may influence the differences.*

ESTJ: *It looks like our differences deal with method of accountability and with emphasis—yours on the people factor, mine on efficiency. Interesting how consistent that is with the feedback I got on that 360 survey—that I need to pay more attention to the human issues.*

ENFP: *I also note your reminder that we have to budget and justify expenses to the organization as a whole.*

ESTJ: *You got that right!*

ENFP: *And my last performance review made it clear I need to present more detailed budgets with project proposals. So . . . let's brainstorm some ways we could accommodate your concerns and mine at the same time.*

STEP 6: *Generate as many potential solutions as possible that will accommodate both sets of needs (including type differences). Review the options to see if type preferences have been accommodated. Discuss and jointly rank the options in order of priority.*

ENFP: *For starters, each employee is allowed up to two weeks a month of telecommuting, the weeks to be staggered so all are not off-site at the same time.*

ESTJ: *O.K., say telecommuting is allowed, but employees must be in the office at least two days each week. And except for emergencies, each employee maintains a predictable, shared schedule whether in the office or off-site. I would consider telecommuting option offered on a three-month trial basis—to be carefully reviewed by management.*

ENFP: *I agree; an option on a three-month trial basis—to be carefully reviewed by both management and staff. Telecommuting is an option during this period. Allow each individual to decide when to work off-site and when to work in the office.*

ESTJ: *Telecommuting could be offered as an incentive to be awarded with a high performance review. And let's not forget we could simply keep things the way they are. Or rather than telecommuting, we go to flextime with the option of a 4-day week.*

ENFP: *We've got ideas to work with. Have we accommodated type differences adequately? For example, I would assume an ST concern deals with measurement of effect and also with the time accountability issue you mentioned.*

ESTJ: *Well, if we do experiment with telecommuting, then we could consider introducing electronic project timesheets to be completed daily to allow for effective supervision of time allocation to specific projects.*

And I think we need to accommodate an ST concern for anticipating problems and working out procedural issues before implementing—as well as doing a careful analysis of the cost/benefit ratio with some kind of review.

ENFP: *I think we're including NF concerns about the effect on people and offering minimal supervision. I also feel we need to give people a sense of freedom to work in their own styles with whatever we opt for.*

ESTJ: *So if we narrow the field, I'd recommend we eliminate the staggered once-a-month weeks. Too unwieldy to implement.*

ENFP: *I agree, and I recommend eliminating the high performance reward. Seems like that would damage collegiality.*

ESTJ: *So that gets us down to options dealing with issues of amount of time spent telecommuting versus time in the office, along with practical issues of time billable to specific projects, accessibility to other staff, a trial period, and a review process. And there's the option still of offering flextime.*

STEP 7: *Devise a plan for implementation (write it down!) and evaluation (set a follow-up date!).*

> **ENFP:** *Would you buy into the idea of our exploring the extent of staff interest in maintaining our current structure, going to flextime, having the option for some form of telecommuting, or even having a "cafeteria" of choices? I've perceived a need that may be only a limited one.*

> **ESTJ:** *Yes, I will buy. Could you meet tomorrow at 1:00 to work out the logistics of this first step? If there is sufficient interest expressed, we can form a task force representative of both management and staff to research all the angles and develop a solid proposal. Meanwhile, I'll write up a summary of our discussion to date and e-mail it to you.*

> **ENFP:** *See you at 1:00. I'll give some thought to how we might develop a needs assessment.*

APPENDIX: A JUNGIAN PERSPECTIVE ON RESPONSE TO THE STRESS INHERENT IN CONFLICT

A brief word about Jungian psychology may help us grasp how the types tend to behave under the stress of conflict. Jung's premise is that our whole "self" consists of both our conscious and unconscious sides.

Our ego, as the focal point of our conscious side, is the way we know ourselves to be. It is the knowledge we possess regarding both the positive and negative aspects of our traits, values, and beliefs.

The opposite of all our self-awareness is part of our shadow side, our unconscious—the flip side of who we know ourselves to be.

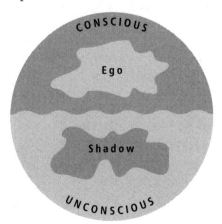

If our hard wiring is allowed to play itself out naturally in our life experiences, and we basically find acceptance for ourselves as we naturally are, then our dominant and auxiliary (first and second) functions are a significant part of our ego. These are the two functions on which our egos most rely to develop perceptions and make judgments. The third and fourth functions of our type are more a part of our shadow side, serving in a supporting role to our ego, gradually developing more into consciousness over our lifespan.

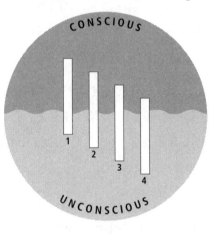

When all is going well, we generally are able to use all four of the mental functions in both extraverted and introverted forms—even if not equally. We apply whichever one is called for in the particular moment or situation. The case history detailed in this appendix will illustrate what happens when we are *not* able to access all four functions.

> Marvin (ESTJ) is an area manager for an automobile parts company. Marvin prided himself on working both efficiently and collaboratively with his store managers. He monitored sales performance of the individual outlets but gave the local managers considerable leeway to set their own quotas. Any differences with staff members were discussed until a mutually satisfying solution was found. His attitude and behavior reflected appropriate use of all four mental functions.

When conflict occurs and our ego feels threatened and the autonomic fight/flight response kicks in, we do what is natural to do—we go to our strength to gain some equilibrium. In type terms, this means we go to our dominant function—and we hold fast to it.

Since our original position in a conflict is usually arrived at with the use of the two functions that are part of our ego, we hold even stronger to that position. When we have difficulty carrying out or convincing others of the "rightness" of our position, then we try harder to do so. The intent is a good one—our ego genuinely believes that its position is best for the occasion. Our ego also loses sight of its blind spots that may involve the third and fourth functions in our type hierarchy.

> With a slump in sales revenue from his area due to a severe economic downturn and pressure from the home office to improve the bottom line, Marvin, now under greater stress, announced major changes with little or no input from the store managers who reported to him. He began to implement decisions made unilaterally with little or no explanation, including a new policy of set quotas for each store. His dominant function of Thinking was working virtually alone.

Extraverts tend to intensify Extraversion in an escalating conflict situation because their dominant function is used mainly in the extraverted attitude. Voice and body get more and more demonstrative. The ego's positive intent is to defend the "right" position in the outer environment where the ego derives its energy. As a result, the third and fourth functions retreat deeper into the unconscious shadow side and are not easily retrieved for fuller perception and judgment.

> When morale suffered and some of Marvin's managers left the firm to work elsewhere, sales figures plummeted even further. In response, Marvin became even more controlling and openly critical of individual managers' performance. With his functions of Intuition and Feeling less accessible to his conscious mind, he was oblivious to the fact that his employees avoided interacting with him unless it was absolutely necessary.

Introverts intensify Introversion and retreat more frequently to their inner world, since this is the environment of their dominant function, removing themselves further and further from extraverted interaction. Again, these behaviors serve a purpose—to protect the "rightness" of the position in the inner environment where the ego is most energized. To the extent that Introverts continue to extravert, it is usually through their auxiliary function. But that function may get increasingly exaggerated as the stress continues. The third and fourth functions retreat deeper into the unconscious, shadow side and are difficult to retrieve for more complete perception and judgment. Extraverts tend to be aware they are voicing their opinion more rigidly. Introverts may act these out in their extraverted environment completely out of their own awareness.

> As pressure from the home office built, Marvin's vocal attacks on his managers extended to his assistant John, an ISTJ. Initially, John saw that Marvin was driving away his most experienced employees, who knew their local markets and were in a good position to do some strategic problem solving with Marvin. However, Marvin rebuffed John's perspective in an early discussion, and John made the decision to go about his own work as inconspicuously as possible. Any criticism of events was now made indirectly to others rather than discussed directly with Marvin.

Characteristics of Types under Limited Stress

In practical terms, the types under limited stress often begin to frustrate the other party as they exhibit some of the following behaviors.

ISJ: Withdraw into excessive gathering and processing of facts and details that support their positions with lessened awareness of how their behaviors are having an impact on other people involved or on the task at hand.

INJ: Withdraw into a dream world of possibilities that become increasingly eccentric and limited and removed from reality.

ITP: Possess less clarity on an issue; have less certainty about their positions but work harder to justify them rather than open their minds to new ideas or information.

IFP: Experience some confusion about the value of what has previously been held most dear and begin to question how they and others are living life.

ETJ: Grow impatient with new information or ideas and push harder to implement their position with no modification.

EFJ: Work harder to maintain agreement between themselves and other people by forcefully pressing an issue, unaware of how this behavior actually puts people off and leads to even less interpersonal connection.

ESP: Increase their attempts to "fix" a situation in different ways or argue a point from a variety of viewpoints, many of which are unrealistic.

ENP: Lose themselves in a stream of consciousness of ideas with little awareness of what is important to the other party.

Characteristics of Types under Extreme Stress

All of these behaviors typically increase the conflict, which, of course, increases the stress. As the stress increases, or if we are particularly fatigued, ill, or under the influence of some kind of substance that makes us less alert and in control of ourselves, then the less conscious functions (and particularly the fourth function) erupt out of the unconscious along with other aspects of the shadow and take control of the ego (Quenk 1984).

Now rather than serve as a support, that function takes over our thoughts and behaviors, expressing itself in exaggerated negative form. It often gets projected onto other people in the form of blame, which we may express vocally or silently. The behavior in the conflict begins to look more like the following:

ISJ: Impulsively carry out or talk about ideas with little thought of the consequences; see a danger or dark side to any possibility outside of their positions.

INJ: Obsess over a particular fact or occurrence or engage in excessive physical behavior as the conflict persists.

ITP: Become hypercritical of the person as well as an idea or feel very sorry for themselves and become unexpectedly emotional, believing the other person doesn't care for them.

IFP: Lose faith in their competence to accomplish anything at the same time they attempt to exert more control over the situations at hand.

ETJ: Internally become less certain of the value of their positions and either withdraw, feeling unappreciated for their efforts, or make adamant statements that even they realize are illogical.

EFJ: Try harder to convince themselves and the other party of the logic of their positions, all the while becoming more illogical; or verbally attack the other party in personal ways and look to a third party for solutions to the conflicts.

ESP: Attribute sinister intentions to the expressions and behaviors of the other party or see dire possibilities of a cosmic nature in suggested solutions.

ENP: Identify and obsess over one fact brought up by or one particular behavior of the other party, seeing it as totally negative; or withdraw into dejection, refusing to become engaged in problem resolution.

Any of these behaviors are clues to take a break from the immediate situation and rest or engage in a different activity to regain equilibrium of the functions. (Readers interested in exploring more about the inferior function will benefit from reading *Was That Really Me?* by Naomi Quenk, who has written in depth about this important aspect of type.) The good news is that once we regain a calm balance, accepting our embarrassing negative behavior as part of our dark side makes it less likely we will repeat the behavior. Simply put, we learn from our mistakes and are thus better able to allow others to do the same.

REFERENCES AND BIBLIOGRAPHY

Blake, R. and J. Mouton. 1964. *The Managerial Grid.* Houston TX: Gulf.

CBS Fox Video. 1991. *The War of the Roses.* 20th Century Fox Film Corp.

Cloke, K. and J. Goldsmith. 2000. *Resolving Conflicts at Work.* San Francisco: Jossey-Bass.

Dana, D. 2001. *Conflict Resolution.* New York: McGraw Hill.

Donohue, W. A. and R. Kolt. 1992. *Managing Interpersonal Conflict.* Newbury Park: Sage Publications.

Domenici, K. 1996. *Mediation—Empowerment in Conflict Management.* Prospect Heights IL: Waveland Press Inc.

Fisher, R. and W. Ury. 1991. *Getting to Yes: Negotiating Agreement Without Giving In.* New York: Penguin Books.

Hammer, A., ed. 1996. *MBTI Applications.* Palo Alto CA: Consulting Psychologists Press, Inc.

Hocker, J. and W. Wilmot. *Interpersonal Conflict.* 3rd ed. Dubuque IA: Wm. C. Brown. 1991.

Johnson, A. 1997. Conflict-Handling Intentions and the MBTI: A Construct Validity. *Journal of Psychological Type* 43: 29–39.

Jung, C. G. 1921/1976. Psychological Types. In *Collected Works.* Vol. 6. Translated by R. F. C. Hull. Princeton, NJ: Princeton University Press.

Lawrence, G. 1993. *People Types & Tiger Stripes.* Gainesville FL: Center for Application of Psychological Type.

McCaulley, M. 1987. Personal communication.

Myers, I. with P. Myers. 1995. *Gifts Differing.* Palo Alto CA: Consulting Psychologists Press, Inc.

Nash, J. F. 1996. *Essays on Game Theory.* Brookfield VT: Edward Elgar Publishing Co.

Paul, J. and M. Paul. 1983. *Do I Have to Give Up Me in Order to Be Loved by You?* Minneapolis MN: CompCare Publishers.

Percival, T., V. Smitheram, and M. Kelly. 1992. Myers-Briggs Type Indicator and Conflict-Handling Intention: An Interactive Approach. *Journal of Psychological Type* 23: 10-16.

Quenk, A. 1984. *Psychological Type and Psychotherapy.* Gainesville FL: Center for Application of Psychological Type

Quenk, N. 2000. *In the Grip: Understanding Type, Stress and the Inferior Function.* Palo Alto CA: Consulting Psychologists Press, Inc.

Quenk, N. 2001. *Was That Really Me?: How Everyday Stress Brings Out Our Hidden Personality.* Palo Alto CA: Consulting Psychologists Press, Inc.

Tieger, P. and B. Barron-Tieger. 2000. *Just Your Type: Create the Relationship You've Always Wanted Using the Secrets of Personality Type.* Boston MA: Little, Brown and Company.

Thomas, K. 2002. *Introduction to Conflict Management.* Palo Alto CA: Consulting Psychologists Press Inc.

Ury, W. 1993. *Getting Past No: Negotiating Your Way From Confrontation To Cooperation.* New York: Bantam Books.

VanSant, S. and D. Payne. 1995. *Psychological Type in Schools: Applications for Educators.* Gainesville FL: Center for Application of Psychological Type.

ABOUT THE AUTHOR

Sondra VanSant, a Licensed Professional Counselor, has spent more than twenty years helping individuals, couples, families, and work teams resolve conflict.

In addition to her clinical mental health and career counseling practice, Sondra does consulting for private corporations, federal and state government agencies, and public school systems in the areas of conflict management, leadership development, communication effectiveness, stress management, career development, and team building.

Sondra is the co-author of *Psychological Type in Schools: Applications for Educators*, also published by CAPT. She resides in Chapel Hill, North Carolina.